Urban Battle Fields of South Asia

Lessons Learned from Sri Lanka, India, and Pakistan

C. Christine Fair

Prepared for the United States Army

 RAND ARROYO CENTER

The research described in this report was sponsored by the United States Army under Contract No. DASW01-01-C-0003.

Library of Congress Cataloging-in-Publication Data

Fair, C. Christine.
   Urban battle fields of South Asia : lessons learned from Sri Lanka, India, and Pakistan / C. Christine Fair.
     p. cm.
   "MG-210."
   Includes bibliographical references.
   ISBN 0-8330-3682-3 (pbk.)
   1. Urban warfare—Sri Lanka. 2. Urban warfare—India. 3. Urban warfare—Pakistan. 4. Terrorism—Sri Lanka—Prevention. 5. Terrorism—India—Prevention. 6. Terrorism—Pakistan—Prevention. 7. War on Terrorism, 2001– I. Title.

U167.5.S7F35 2004
355.4'26'0954—dc22

                                       2004019129

The RAND Corporation is a nonprofit research organization providing objective analysis and effective solutions that address the challenges facing the public and private sectors around the world. RAND's publications do not necessarily reflect the opinions of its research clients and sponsors.

RAND® is a registered trademark.

Published 2004 by the RAND Corporation
1776 Main Street, P.O. Box 2138, Santa Monica, CA 90407-2138
1200 South Hayes Street, Arlington, VA 22202-5050
201 North Craig Street, Suite 202, Pittsburgh, PA 15213-1516
RAND URL: http://www.rand.org/
To order RAND documents or to obtain additional information, contact
Distribution Services: Telephone: (310) 451-7002;
Fax: (310) 451-6915; Email: order@rand.org

Preface

Over the past several years, the U.S. military has become increasingly interested in military operations in urban areas. This attention is warranted because such operations are among the most complex challenges that confront the U.S. Army, be it a conventional conflict or military operations other than war. Recent Army experiences in Iraq demonstrate the ability of the adversary to engage U.S. forces in urbanized areas to vitiate much of the U.S. military's edge in high-technology firepower. The likelihood that U.S. forces will engage in these environments will only increase as societies continue to urbanize.

Compared to a number of other nations, the Army has relatively less experience operating in this environment. There are countries that have been immersed in urban internal security and peace operations for decades. This report will look at three such states: Sri Lanka, India, and Pakistan. While the three countries lack the technological sophistication and resources of U.S. armed forces, their experiences may be illuminating because of their extensive encounters with such conflicts. Moreover, they have had to find means of countering the urban threat within severe budget constraints.

This monograph will analyze cases involving sustained campaigns of urban terrorism that have occurred in Sri Lanka, India, and Pakistan. It will identify key innovations of the organizations using terrorism. It will also detail the three states' responses to the evolving threats they confront, noting successful as well as unsuccessful efforts. This effort will specifically focus upon the *operational* and *tactical* aspects of the selected campaigns. It will not address the political, economic and sociological dimensions of these cases, which have been amply addressed by the literature on these conflicts.

This monograph has several purposes. First, it seeks to garner operational insights from the experiences of countries that may enhance the Army's ability to operate in the urban environment. Second, it identifies common structural similarities within the militant organizations in question that might be targeted to degrade their ability to project power. Third, as these states are all partners to various extents in the global war on terrorism, this report describes ways to improve security cooperation programs with these states. Finally, it lists key insights from these countries that may inform U.S. stability operations in Afghanistan, Iraq, and future operations.

This research is a part of a larger effort led by RAND Arroyo Center to identify current U.S. force requirements for urban contingency planning and to develop innovative approaches for doing so. This monograph will be of interest to individuals within the government whose responsibilities include doctrine, policy designs, planning, and preparation to support civil or military operation in urban environments. It will also be of interest to individuals interested in structural features of organizations using terrorism to achieve their objectives.

Research in conjunction with this report was undertaken for the U.S. Army Training and Doctrine Command (TRADOC) and was conducted in RAND Arroyo Center's Force Development and Technology Program. RAND Arroyo Center, part of the RAND Corporation, is a federally funded research and development center sponsored by the United States Army.

For more information on RAND Arroyo Center, contact the Director of Operations (telephone 310-393-0411, extension 6419; FAX 310-451-6952; e-mail Marcy_Agmon@rand.org), or visit Arroyo's web site at http://www.rand.org/ard/.

Contents

CHAPTER THREE

CHAPTER FOUR

Figures

Tables

Summary

Sri Lanka, India, and Pakistan all have extensive experience in dealing with militant groups that employ violence to achieve their objectives. Although much of this experience has been gained in rural or jungle terrain, all three states have wrestled with terrorism in urban environments as well. This research assesses several sustained campaigns of urban violence in South Asia to draw out the evolution of groups employing terrorism and to exposit the way in which each state attempted to counter the ever-changing threat.

The lessons learned from the manifestations of urban terrorism are numerous. First, this exercise illuminated numerous structural similarities among groups that use terror as an instrument within the three states considered. For example, most have developed globalized networks to support their operations and sustain their organization. Second, the United States is currently engaged with these states in the global war on terrorism in various capacities and through differing means. Understanding the internal security dynamics of Sri Lanka, India, and Pakistan as well as the challenges they confront should offer insights into the types of engagement that might be useful to both parties. These observations should also inform the expectations of the United States as to the limits of the possible within the region. Third, the population terrain[1] of each of these countries is richly complex

---

[1] The notion of population terrain used here reflects the work of Vijay Madan (1997). Madan writes that "Population should be considered in the same manner as terrain is in any military planning and appreciations . . . . [An] examination of the 'population terrain' factor would lead to deducing the important segments of the population which must be dominated

and marked by religious-sectarian distinctions as well as ethnic and cultural differences. Some of the methods developed to manage the urban threat may provoke thoughts about U.S.-led stability operations in countries that are similarly diverse in social structure. Some of the key findings of this report are summarized below.

Structural Similarities: Insights for the War on Terrorism

Nearly every nonstate actor discussed in this study has established transnational networks to facilitate the movement of, *inter alia,* money, information, weapons and other war materiel, as well as persons. These networks are used to raise funds as well—through both licit and illicit means. Their web of relationships also permits different groups to interact and cross-fertilize. Afghanistan, the Middle East, India, the countries of Europe, Southeast Asia, the United Kingdom, and the United States have all served as meeting places for these militant organizations. The cross-fertilization of militant groups underscores the importance of understanding the best practices of terror utilization, as other groups employing terror are likely to take advantage of this knowledge. These networks can also be used to encourage co-ethnics and co-religionists spread throughout the diaspora to espouse particular movements' causes. Co-ethnics and co-religionists living in the West have been able to exploit the political systems there to create environments that are favorable to their movement's objectives. One of the key institutions in these trans-state networks is the university. Universities emerge as important sources of manpower as well as technical expertise. While the international community understands the financial aspects of these networks, it is less clear how much attention other dimensions receive.

This report also finds several common weaknesses within the states that these groups exploit, such as the lack of communication

---

and which . . . could be ignored or handled in a latter time frame. The insurgents too, from the very start of their movement, endeavor to dominate the 'population terrain' and usually score over the [counterintelligence] forces, who start on the wrong foot by expending all their energies and resources on trying to dominate only the insurgents."

and intelligence sharing across jurisdictional lines of police and other authorities. Limiting terrorist groups' power projection requires a coherent state response that incorporates national and local law enforcement and intelligence entities. It requires that intelligence flow up and down between the central and local authorities as well as horizontally among and between various law enforcement and intelligence groups within the state and federal sectors. Groups also exploit the lack of language assets within the state security apparatus. The Sri Lankan army, police, and intelligence agencies have very few Tamil language interpreters. Diasporan organizations operating in the United States have the advantage of languages that are "low density" (e.g., languages for which the U.S. military and law enforcement have few assets).

Finally, all groups exploit fissures in the relationship that develops between the populace and the law enforcement authorities. As security breaks down and the people no longer have trust in the government, citizens do not cooperate with the authorities. Further, these case studies illuminate the fundamental role of local police forces and the importance of ensuring that their training and equipment is adequate to the task they face.

Security Cooperation: Implications for U.S. Engagement of Sri Lanka, India, and Pakistan

The United States currently has counterterrorism and law enforcement working groups with India and Pakistan. These programs, with varying concentration, focus on the integration of intelligence, law enforcement, legal, and diplomatic aspects of the fight against terrorism. This analysis found that these efforts to fortify all aspects of these states' internal security apparatus are critical to ensuring that these states can function as effective partners in the war on terrorism.

This analysis also found that all three states demonstrate poor coordination across the myriad state and federal agencies. (The United States too faces this complex challenge.) This finding may inform the United States in its counterterrorism partnerships with each of these countries. For instance, which U.S. entities should be engaged in security cooperation programs with India, Pakistan, and Sri Lanka, and which agencies within these countries should be included?

Finally, it is possible that some of the operational lessons learned by these three states as they confronted their own cases of militancy may have value to the U.S. forces in their current and future urban challenges. All of these states are complex societies with richly diverse populations. Some of the empirical evidence garnered from Pakistan's Islamicized community-policing model and Sri Lanka's vigilance committees may offer some insight for U.S. police operations in similarly complex social environments.

Acknowledgments

Dr. Russell Glenn has been a source of wisdom, guidance, and inspiration. I am grateful to Dr. Glenn for believing in this project and obtaining funding to execute it. His advice has enhanced its value. I am also indebted to many Foreign Army Area Officers of the U.S. Army who have been a constant source of insight and knowledge. Colonel Richard Girven, the current Defense Attaché in Colombo, has been generous with his time during this project as well as several other projects at RAND. Colonel Girven arranged numerous meetings in Sri Lanka, without which the chapter on that country would have been far less interesting. In addition, the Operations Coordinator of the DAO Office in Colombo, IS1 Albert G. Dobias, imparted a wealth of information about the Tamil Tigers. Colonel Steven Sboto has been a vast resource in understanding the capabilities of the Indian army and the threat with which it must contend. Also, Dr. Ajai Sahni of the Institute of Conflict Management in New Delhi has been tremendously helpful in arranging a broad swath of meetings with India's key internal security managers. I am particularly grateful to all of the officers of the Punjab police who were generous with their time. Colonel Dave Smith, who was the Army Attaché in Islamabad until quite recently, has provided key observations about Pakistan and its internal security challenges for years. I am also thankful to all of the journalists and analysts in Pakistan who spent time with me on and off the record. I owe a special thanks to my mentors Ashley Tellis and Colonel Jack Gill, who diligently and insightfully reviewed an earlier draft of this document. Their numerous keen suggestions have made this a much stronger analytical product. I also would like to thank Yuna Huh, who read an early version of this draft and provided very helpful suggestions to improve upon it. Despite the efforts of all of these individuals, any and all deficiencies in this product are the sole responsibility of the author.

Glossary

AISSF	All India Sikh Student Federation
AK-47	Automatic Kalashnikov, Model 1947
BSF	Border Security Force
CA	Civil Affairs
CRPF	Central Reserve Police Force
DEA	Drug Enforcement Administration
DIG	Deputy Inspector General
DII	Directorate of Internal Intelligence
EPRLF	Eelam Peoples' Revolutionary Liberation Front
EROS	Eelam Revolutionary Organizers
FTO	Foreign Terrorist Organization
GSL	Government of Sri Lanka
IED	Improvised Explosive Device
IG	Inspector General
IPKF	Indian Peacekeeping Force
ISI	Inter-Services Intelligence Directorate (Pakistan)
JM	Jaish-e-Mohammed ("Army of Mohammed")
JVP	Janatha Vimukthi Peramuna (a.k.a. "People's Liberation Front")

KCF	Khalistan Commando Force
Kfir	Israeli Built Aircraft
KLF	Khalistan Liberation Force
LeJ	Lashkar-e-Jhangvi ("Army of Jhang")
LeT	Lashkar-e-Taibba ("Army of the Pure")
LTTE	Liberation Tigers of Tamil Eelam (a.k.a. "Tamil Tigers")
MQM	Muttehida Qaumi Movement ("United National Movement"; formerly Muhajir Qaumi Movement, or "Migrants National Movement")
NGO	Nongovernmental Organization
PFLP	Popular Front for the Liberation of Palestine
PKK	Kurdistan Workers' Party
PLOTE	People's Liberation Organization for Tamil Eelam
PSYOP	Psychological Operations
RAW	Research and Analysis Wing
RDX	Royal Demolition eXplosive; 1,3,5-trinitro-1,3,5-triazine (a.k.a. cyclonite or hexogen)
SB	Special Branch (in Pakistan and Sri Lanka)
SGPC	Shiromani Gurdwara Prabandhak Committee
SLA	Sri Lankan Army
SMP	Sipah-e-Muhammed Pakistan ("Army of Muhammed")
SSP	Sipah-e-Sahaba-e-Pakistan ("Guardians of the Friends of the Prophet")
TELO	Tamil Eelam Liberation Organization
TJP	Tehrik-e-Jaffria Pakistan ("Movement of Followers of the Jaffria sect (Fiqah-e-Jaffria)")

TNFJ	Tehrik-e-Nifaz-e-Fiqah-e-Jaffria ("Movement for the Implementation of the Jaffria Sect")
TULF	Tamil United Liberation Front
VC	Vigilance Committee

CHAPTER ONE

Introduction

Background

India, Pakistan, and Sri Lanka comprise three important states of South Asia. All have extensive experience with confronting civilian militant groups and criminal organizations that employ violence for various political, economic, and organizational ends. These states, particularly India and Sri Lanka, have contended, to varying degrees, with organized campaigns of violence in rural and jungle areas. For example, India has been struggling with insurgency in the dense jungle terrain of its northeast. Sri Lanka has also fought the Liberation Tigers of Tamil Eelam (LTTE, also known as the Tamil Tigers) in the jungle terrain of the Jaffna Peninsula that forms the northern third of the island nation.

However, all three states have also had to wrestle with the *urban* manifestation of organized violence. India has been forced to contend with low-intensity conflict in the Punjab, Jammu, and Kashmir and high-intensity crime in the densely populated cities of Delhi and Mumbai. India has also faced an ongoing low-intensity conflict with militant elements in the Kashmiri city of Srinagar since 1989. Sri Lanka has been facing ongoing threats from the ferocious and highly competent LTTE in built-up areas as well as the jungle. The LTTE has perpetrated dozens of attacks in the capital city of Colombo as well as in the ideological capital of Tamil Eelam (the Tamil homeland), Jaffna. Pakistan has been battling, with various degrees of dedication, forms of violence that are almost exclusively urban phenomena: sectarian violence between militarized Shi'a and Sunni organizations as well as the antistate activities of the ethnonationalist organization the Muttehida Qaumi Movement (MQM), formerly known as the Muhajir Qaumi Movement.

This monograph will explore urban violence in these three countries as employed by a variety of militarized organizations, irrespective of whether they are referred to as "terrorist" or "insurgent."[1] Generally speaking, we will consider the application of terrorism and the state response that together comprise low-intensity conflict. As will be apparent, many of these militant groups engage in high-intensity criminal activity to sustain themselves at some point in their institutional development.[2] Such groups may behave like organized criminal outfits (e.g., they criminalize) or may cooperate and even collaborate with established criminal syndicates.[3]

Methodology

Case Selection

Pakistan, India, and Sri Lanka have encountered violence of various types in their urban areas for decades. This may include random violence, bombs in markets, burning down cinemas, and so forth. Examining every sort of urban violence and state response is not feasible within the constraints of this effort, which is limited to include only

---

[1] This work does not address the important question of the ways in which insurgent movements differ from terrorist movements. This analysis concedes that the meaningful distinctions between "insurgents" and "terrorists" do not form the subject of serious inquiry in the post-9/11 analysis of political violence, and that efforts to argue for such distinctions are often met with scorn from policymakers, political leaders, intelligence analysts, and law enforcement officials. For reasons of political and diplomatic expediency, many countries have deftly achieved the reclassification of "insurgent" groups as terrorists as a quid pro quo for recognizing the terrorist threat of peer states. For example, the United States became much more willing to see Chechnya as a theater of terrorism to attain Russia's participation in its global war on terrorism.

[2] For a more detailed discussion of the structural features of organized crime, see Gunaratna (2000d), P. Singh (2000), and Sarkar and Tiwari (2002). High-intensity crime differs from low-level crime in both the degree and scale of operations and coordination.

[3] Prakash Singh (2000) uses the term "high-intensity crime" to emphasize these dimensions of organized crime within the Indian context.

sustained campaigns of urban violence by groups operating within the countries in question.

Our study of Pakistan, for example, does not examine the activities of groups operating in Indian-held Kashmir and the Indian hinterland even though they are based in Pakistan or Pakistan-held Kashmir.[4] These groups have not launched sustained campaigns in the cities of Pakistan, and the state has not taken significant efforts to restrict them, because they comprise part of Pakistan's strategy of proxy war in India. Therefore, it makes little sense in the context of this report to focus on these groups within the context of Pakistan.

It is not yet clear whether these militant outfits and their activities should form the subject of study within the India chapter. While some of them have allegedly struck deep within India, it is too soon to determine whether or not their attacks constitute sustained campaigns of urban violence. While these organizations have operated for several years in the Kashmiri city of Srinagar, the author has dealt with these militants in the Srinagar theater and the concomitant response of the Indian security forces in a previous study (Fair, 2002).

Therefore, the chapter on Pakistan will focus upon the sectarian and MQM-related violence that has plagued major Pakistani cities in Sindh and the Punjab since the early 1980s. This is an area of which Pakistan's own military, policy, and academic communities have written at length and a segment of urban violence against which Pakistan has been able to achieve some degree of success.

India too has faced very well organized, widely backed, and exceptionally well-financed adversaries and continues to do so to date. India has experienced high-profile attacks in New Delhi in which the alleged perpetrators were the Pakistan-backed Lashkar-e-Taibba and Jaish-e-Mohammed. While these attacks were singularly significant,

---

[4] This term is preferred to describe that portion of Kashmir which is held by Pakistan, rather than the politically charged alternatives of "Azad Kashmir" ("Free Kashmir"), used by proponents of Islamabad's position, or Pakistan-Occupied Kashmir, used by those who support New Delhi's stance. Similarly, when describing that portion of Kashmir administered by India, the term "Indian-held Kashmir" is used in preference to "Indian-Occupied Kashmir," which implies acceptance of Pakistan's contention, or "Kashmir," which suggests that there is no dispute over the disposition of the territory, which is India's preferred nomenclature.

officials in Delhi see them as isolated, independent strikes. India has experienced a number of sustained urban campaigns, the most notorious and lethal of which was the Sikh insurgency in the Punjab. Therefore, the Sikh militancy and the corresponding response of the state security apparatus will comprise the major Indian case in this report. This analysis will particularly focus upon Punjab insurgency in the wake of the 1984 raid of militants housed in the sacred Sikh shrine, the Golden Temple.[5]

Sri Lanka has been battling a fierce ethnic Tamil insurgency for decades. In the initial years, there were a number of Tamil militant organizations that took up arms in pursuit of Tamil liberation. At present, the main organization is the LTTE. Since early 2002 there has been a ceasefire, although its fate appears to be uncertain. Sri Lankan authorities were very forthcoming during fieldwork in that country. The Tamil insurgency, particularly the LTTE's role, and the state's response will comprise the case study for that country.

Analytical Tools and Methods

This effort employs a combination of analytical tools and methods. First, the author has conducted an extensive literature review of cases identified for this study, focusing on tactical and operational aspects. Consistent with this objective, the author perused the standard security, academic, and military literature through electronic databases. However, as many of the defense periodicals of the countries in question are not available through such indexes or through the Internet, the author visited the University of California Berkeley research library, which houses one of the most extensive South Asia collections in the United States. (Unfortunately, although Sri Lanka's staff college does produce a military journal, it is not widely available outside of Sri Lanka and we were unable to locate it within the United

---

[5] This monograph does not treat pre–Operation Bluestar militancy in Punjab. There is little doubt that this phase of the militancy is important, but data on its tactical and operational aspects are not abundant. Individuals interviewed in India were also unable to provide adequate information about that phase of India's counterinsurgency operation. The author recognizes that this paucity of data constitutes a potential weakness of this current effort.

States.)[6] The author also obtained materials during numerous field-trips to the region that would ordinarily be difficult to acquire.

Second, the author has established other contacts with political analysts at the American embassies located in these three countries and within other relevant U.S. agencies.

Third, the author made several trips to the region in the course of this research: three trips to India (two in the fall of 2002 and one in the spring of 2003); two trips to Pakistan in January and August 2003; and one trip to Sri Lanka in November 2002. In addition, the material here draws from interviews conducted during a December 2000 research trip to Pakistan for a previous research effort (see Tellis, Fair, Medby, 2001).

The author met extensively with retired and active military personnel, officers in the police forces and police intelligence agencies, and with civilian analysts, journalists, and observers. Each person interviewed was explicitly told that this research was being conducted for a project funded by the U.S. government. Participants were told that they would not be directly cited. In many cases, the specific way in which interlocutors are identified in this report was negotiated between the respondent and the author. The author, when requested, sent the conversation transcript to the interviewee for verification and excision of material deemed too sensitive to publish. As some of these individuals are targets of militant organizations, their safety and anonymity remain the highest priority.

Objectives and Implications of This Study

This current effort analyzes the tactical and operational aspects of the identified cases of sustained campaigns of urban violence in Sri Lanka, Pakistan, and India. It seeks to identify key innovations employed by militant outfits. This monograph also exposits both suc-

---

[6] Because tactical and operational information on these cases is relatively rare, the citation base does not reflect the extent to which the literature was reviewed. In contrast, information about the social, political, and economic origins of the selected cases is extensive.

cessful and unsuccessful state responses to the operations of these militant groups and their innovations. Needless to say, there are gaps in the available data about the identified cases. In some instances, there is much more information about militant innovation. In other cases, information about state response is more ample. Despite the best efforts of this author to select comparable cases, this problem has not been entirely avoided.

This work is driven by the fundamental judgment that the urban center affords numerous advantages to groups engaging in organized violence. The advantages include employment, cover, a diverse social landscape, anonymity, an in-place support infrastructure, and large audiences for their actions. Elucidating these states' experiences with such phenomena may provide some insight into the ways in which the United States can better operate and counter these developments as it pursues its objectives in the global war on terrorism.

This study of urban political violence in South Asia aims to contribute to understanding the nature of sustained urban violence campaigns in the region. The author anticipates that this study will also contribute to the expertise for dealing with and mitigating the impact of organized violence in urbanized terrain. This study will discuss the relevance of its findings to the United States in general and the armed forces in particular as the United States and its partners attempt to deal with political violence at home and abroad.

Summary of the Findings

Each of the three cases identified demonstrate that there is a linkage between militancy and organized crime, to various extents. This may include overt criminalization, as was the case with the Sikh militancy. It may include networking between militant and criminal organizations for joint utility. Some militancies may retain their fundamental political objectives (e.g., the LTTE) while relying upon combinations of criminal and legal ventures to support their movement.

Each case demonstrates that militant outfits have been very adept at creating and leveraging extensive global networks. These networks are mobilized to raise funds (e.g., from diasporan co-ethnics or co-religionists), to interact with other militant and criminal outfits, and to generate political sympathies among the populace where diasporans reside as well as within the capitals of diasporan settlements.

In at least two of the cases noted here (the Sikh militancy and the Tamil conflict), militant organizations have made extensive use of the university to acquire technical talent and recruit militant manpower as well as ideologues. Universities, located in urbanized areas, have also provided access to urban populations. The university has also been an important node where militant leadership can interact with nongovernmental organizations (NGOs) to manage the perception of the conflict and to ensure that NGOs are favorable toward the arguments advanced by the militants.

The cases of the Sikh militant organizations and the LTTE demonstrate that groups innovate in terms of firepower used and the methods of employment. The LTTE has demonstrated extreme competence in improving the lethality of its suicide vests, employing better explosive devices, and finding new and novel ways of deploying these weapons.

All three states involved have had difficulty in developing effective counterstrategies. India is the only state of the three that can boast of decisively defeating one of its militancies: the Khalistan movement. All three states demonstrate similar problems. For instance, across the cases, local police are totally unprepared for the task at hand. Yet the police are key to combating militancy. The police are poorly trained, lack the most rudimentary investigative capabilities (e.g., collecting and handling evidence), and are poorly equipped. Each of the three countries lacks forensics laboratory capabilities or trained individuals who can exploit the few resources that are available. Intelligence flows tend to be unidirectional, flowing up from local police to the national intelligence and security agencies. This is unfortunate because police, with their local knowledge, could most likely be more effective if intelligence also flowed downward. The judiciary branches, to varying extents, are all deeply flawed in each state. Without a transparent judicial apparatus, fair and open trials are difficult to attain and may encourage less-disciplined police forces to deliver extrajudicial punishment.

Obviously, intelligence is critical to any effective counterstrategy. Gathering high-quality intelligence relies upon robust relations between the police and the populace, which currently is *not* the case in any of the countries examined. Intelligence also needs to be developed from a patient and complex analysis of the population terrain. In each case examined, this has been a problem at least in part because citizens of the countries in question fear the police and avoid any unnecessary interaction with them. One detriment of this dysfunctional relationship between the police and the policed is that citizens are discouraged from reporting suspicious activity to the authorities. Similarly, they may find other means of providing security or resolving disputes that evades police interaction. In some cases (e.g., Sri Lanka), the intelligence and security apparatus lack the requisite language skills to collect and analyze data about the groups in question. Limited experiments with community policing (e.g., in Pakistan) and vigilance committees (in Sri Lanka) provide some data that these problems can be mitigated over time if there is a sincere interest in doing so.

All three cases demonstrate that state counterstrategies are hampered by poor coordination across the myriad state and federal agencies. This finding may have relevance to the United States in its partnerships with each of these countries. What agencies need to be involved for complete effectiveness? Which agencies are capable of interacting with the United States? What training do in-country organizations require to be effective counterterrorism partners of the United States? Understanding the varied country dynamics may enable the United States to better identify which agencies should be included in engagement and which agencies should be targeted for training or other programs to enhance capabilities.

Organization of This Report

The remainder of this report will be organized as follows. The subsequent three chapters expand upon the selected case studies in question for Sri Lanka, India, and Pakistan respectively. The histories included in each section are not meant to be exhaustive; rather, they are intended to give the reader a basic overview of the campaign identified. Each chapter will provide an introduction to the landscape of organized urban violence in the country and identify the particular campaigns that form the basis of the case study. Each will attempt to identify militant innovations in tactics and targeting as well as shifts in organizational composition and objective. Finally, each chapter will detail the state's response, noting successful efforts as well as unsuccessful ones. The final chapter will present a synthesis of case findings, noting the structural similarities that inhere in each as well as observations about the state counterstrategy employed. Because each of these states to varying degrees is a partner in the war on terrorism led by the United States, some of the findings of this report may inform the security relationship that the United States forges with each. Where appropriate and where possible, this chapter will draw out potential implications for the United Sates as it continues to encounter political violence in various environments.

CHAPTER TWO

Sri Lanka

Preview of the Findings

This chapter focuses on the Tamil militancy and in particular on the efforts of the Liberation Tigers of Tamil Eelam (LTTE), also known as the Tamil Tigers. The Tigers, through the course of their some 20 years of operating, have evolved in substantial ways. The LTTE has developed a diverse organizational structure that in many ways resembles a conventional army; it includes several special functions, e.g., an amphibious element (Sea Tigers), a putative airborne group (the Air Tigers), and a suicide force (the Black Tigers). The LTTE also has a specialized intelligence unit as well as a subordinate political wing. The LTTE vigorously recruits female cadres for combat operations as well as for executing suicide attacks. Another notable feature of the LTTE is that it has shown remarkable adaptability to guerilla operations both in jungle and urbanized terrain.

The LTTE has also learned to make effective operational use of noncombatants: fighting cadres are usually accompanied by nearly an equivalent number of unarmed personnel. These "noncombatants" are tasked with carrying away slain LTTE cadres or dressing the dead in civilian dress to give the illusion that the slain were civilians. These persons play an important role in the LTTE's deception campaign.

The LTTE has made substantial improvements in the construction of improvised explosive devices and suicide vests as well as in the operational use of these devices. One of the ways in which the LTTE is able to achieve such innovation is through the use of "outsourcing" to contractors. For example, the LTTE exploits Tamil engineering students at major universities, who may comply out of coercion or out of sympathy toward the movement and its objectives. The LTTE is perhaps most famous for its development of the suicide bomber. It is believed that the LTTE leadership observed the utility of this technique in Beirut and resolved to implement it with substantial improvement. Not only have they made technical enhancements (e.g., lethality radius), they have also learned to take advantage of women in conducting these attacks. Women, for instance, can hide the devices under their saris (the several meters of fabric draped in a dress-like fashion over a blouse and petticoat) in the guise of pregnancy.

Another important evolution of the LTTE is that it has over the years developed into a formidable global operator. This has allowed the LTTE to interact with other militant groups in the Middle East and in South Asia, which has opened up new opportunities for weapons procurement and other necessary operational assets as well as the exchange of "lessons learned" among different groups. The LTTE raises funds through myriad global legal and illegal means and has learned to heavily leverage the Tamil diaspora. In addition, the LTTE's perception management campaign is global in conception and in execution. Until the terrorist attacks against the United States on September 11, 2001 (hereafter, "9/11"), the LTTE was able to leverage diasporan sources of political support to cultivate sympathetic positions within the world capitals. (This dramatically changed in the post-9/11 environment, when most international actors were not keen to distinguish between "insurgencies" and "terrorist outfits.")

The Sri Lankan security force, in lamentable contrast, has had considerable difficulty keeping up with the LTTE. For reasons that are far from clear, the government has not been able to develop a perception management campaign to counter LTTE's own efforts. Nor has the Sri Lankan government been able to mobilize the Sinhalese diaspora to cultivate receptive public opinion toward Colombo's position.

In addition, the Sri Lankan security forces have had difficulty penetrating the cells of the LTTE. This is, at least in part, because the Sri Lankan security forces have relatively few personnel with Tamil language skills. In addition, many of the techniques to counter the LTTE have backfired. For example, the use of static pickets and road blocks has engendered hostility among the innocent Tamils who feel harassed, has yielded little actionable intelligence, and has created a number of targets of opportunity for the LTTE.

The Sri Lankan security forces have also apparently failed to interpret the LTTE's modus operandi of "action and inaction." The LTTE tends to operate by striking and pausing: it rarely conducts two operations within a short period of time. Despite this fairly predicable behavior, the Sri Lankan security forces nonetheless tend to interpret the pause as an abatement of threat.

Moreover, Colombo has not successfully unified the efforts of the various counterintelligence, police, and intelligence organizations. One of the consequences of this is that intelligence tends not to flow from the central intelligence agencies to the police officers. This has apparently hindered police operational capabilities. Sri Lanka's brief experiment with integrating these agencies as well as with community policing (i.e., vigilance committees) appeared to enhance Colombo's ability to interdict LTTE operations.

Finally, Colombo has benefited tremendously by the sensitivity to political violence engendered by the post-9/11 global environment. Tamils abroad, sensitive to the appellation of "terrorist," have pressured the LTTE to pursue a political solution, and the varied international efforts to proscribe the LTTE has made fundraising more difficult. Most importantly, the post-9/11 world is less receptive to nonstate groups seeking to change maps by force. It has also concentrated the attention of the United States and others that the Sri Lankan armed forces need help in combating this formidable adversary on the battlefield even while it episodically seeks a political resolution of outstanding disputes.

Figure 2.1
Map of Sri Lanka

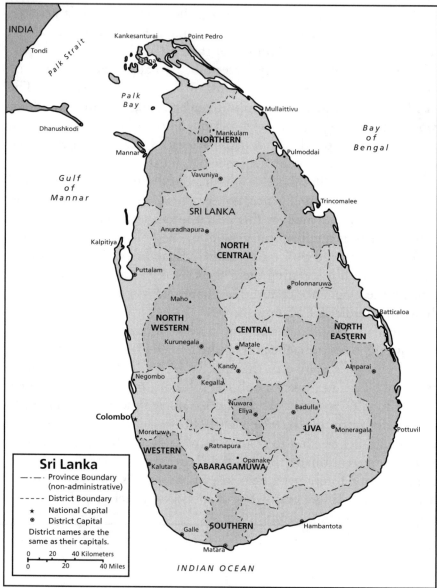

RAND MG210-1

Introduction to the Case

The Tigers are a formidable force. For nearly 20 years they have confounded the Sri Lankan security forces. In addition, the Tigers defeated five divisions of the Indian army that went to Sri Lanka during an operation that was conceived as a peacekeeping operation. (New Delhi and Colombo signed an agreement authorizing the arrival of Indian peacekeeping forces on July 29, 1987.) The Indians soon found that there was in fact no peace to keep and that they had become a party to the conflict. The Indian army, after battling the Tamil Tigers for three long and bloody years, withdrew from the conflict ignominiously on March 24, 1990.[1]

The consequences of the Tamil conflict have been grave when measured in human terms. Some 64,000 people perished between the onset of heightened militancy in 1983 and the cessation of the violence in early 2002. The victims have come from virtually every walk of life, including children and adult civilians (Tamil and non-Tamil), militants, security forces, and politicians.[2]

Understanding how the LTTE, with its relatively small force, was able to withstand two modern-day armed forces should be instructive to analysts of militancies for several reasons. First, the reasons behind the LTTE's success and lethality cast light on other organizations. Second, the Sri Lankan army (SLA) and other security forces have been battling the LTTE for some two decades, and this

---

[1] For a more complete account of the Indian intervention, see Gunaratna (1994), D. Singh (2001), and Bullion (1994).

[2] See Center for Defense Information (2002). The global environment became very hostile to organizations like the LTTE in the aftermath of the terrorist attacks in the United States on September 11, 2001. On December 21, 2001, Ranil Wickremesinghe became Sri Lanka's prime minister following the United National Front coalition's convincing victory over the People's Alliance in the December 2001 parliamentary elections. Wickremesinghe ran on a platform of peace that was in part motivated by the damage inflicted by the LTTE during its audacious attack on Sri Lanka's only international airport in July 2001 (see, for example, Subramanian (2001) and Clark (2002)). As a consequence of the Sri Lankan prime minister's willingness to engage the LTTE as a full partner in peace and as a result of the degraded global environment for LTTE actions, both partners initiated a peace process in December 2001. This culminated in the joint signing of a Memorandum of Understanding between the Sri Lankan government and the LTTE in February 2002.

vast experience provides numerous opportunities to understand what has worked and what has not. Third, militant groups learn from each other. Indian counterterrorism and police personnel allege that the LTTE interacted with Khalistani militants, as will be discussed later in this report. Understanding the panoply of lessons learned from the LTTE is important because future adversaries may also have studied the success of the LTTE.[3] Finally, it is instructive to understand why the LTTE, at the height of its military power, was strategically crippled by the post-9/11 environment and willingly entered into a peace process with Colombo.

Background to the Tamil Militancy

The Tamil insurgency[4] is overwhelmingly an ethnonationalist conflict rooted to Sri Lanka's history of colonization and decolonization.

---

[3] Connor (2002).

[4] While this chapter on Sri Lanka focuses upon the activities of the Tamil Tigers and the state response to the Tamil militancy, it should be noted that this is not the only insurgency that has challenged Colombo. Prior to the widespread outbreak of Tamil ethnonationalist violence, Sri Lanka battled militant forces unleashed by the Janatha Vimukthi Peramuna (JVP) insurrection in 1971. A second wave of JVP violence occurred in the 1980s in response to the rise of Tamil nationalism. The JVP, or "People's Liberation Front," was founded in 1967 as a putatively "Maoist" organization comprised mainly of disaffected Sinhalese students. On April 5, 1971, the JVP launched an ambitious campaign to seize the state apparatus. In doing so it seized numerous police stations in the countryside. Although initially the actions were rural in nature, the insurrection spread to Sri Lanka's urbanized areas. For the first time in post-independence history, the Sri Lankan army was involved in active combat battling its own civilian population. The army restored order within two weeks, by which time over 5,000 had died and some 14,000 Sinhalese were detained in camps. The second wave of JVP activities occurred in the late 1980s as a backlash against the rise of Tamil nationalism. Following the (unsuccessful) Indian peacekeeping operations to wrest Jaffna from the LTTE, the JVP sought to target Sri Lankans who were relatively moderate on the Tamil question. In 1987, a JVP cadre tossed a hand grenade at President Jayawardene and Prime Minister Premdasa. This effort was not successful. In this round of insurrection, the JVP is accused of having killed some 10,000 Sri Lankans between 1987 and 1989 (Connor, 2002, p. 42, citing De Silva, 1998, p. 112). As with the first JVP revolt, the JVP support base was the rural hinterland even though it operated within urban theaters (Perera, 1996). The Sri Lankan security forces crushed this insurrection as they had the first. While the JVP insurrection did provide the Sri Lankan army some degree of "battle inoculation," the army was still completely overwhelmed by the intensity, the longevity, and the

This substantially distinguishes the Tamil uprising from other internal security challenges in South Asia, where militancy has tended to be intertwined with communal (e.g., religious) and sectarian differences. Dating the origin of the conflict is difficult: both scholars of Sri Lankan history and the residents of the island nation themselves tend to disagree on the subject. What is clear is that the island had never before comprised a unified political entity before the arrival of the British.[5]

Under British governance, South Indians were brought to Sri Lanka as bonded laborers for the coffee plantations and tea estates. Although most of these individuals were ethnic Tamils from what is the present-day state of Tamilnadu in India, others came from the modern-day Indian states of Kerala, Karnataka, and Andhra Pradesh. In 1833, the British consolidated the entire island within a unified administrative structure, which marked the establishment of Sri Lanka as a modern state. British development efforts focused on the central and western areas of the island, thereby leaving out the Tamils, who were concentrated in the north and northeast. In response to this exclusion, the Tamils pursued education in American and British missionary schools, which enabled the English-educated Tamils to participate in the offices of government administration. Thus, at the time of Sri Lankan independence in 1948, the Tamils enjoyed substantial representation in the apparatus of state despite their minority status.[6]

---

effectiveness of the Tamil militancy that followed. See United States Institute of Peace (2001), "JVP Uprising," available at Sri Lanka Army Online, http://202.51.141.138/ Operations.htm, last accessed June 26, 2003. Also see Chandraprema (1991). Despite Colombo's extensive experiences battling the JVP in both the 1970s and 1980s, the Sri Lankan security forces continue to have difficulty in countering the LTTE.

[5] There was no coherent political structure uniting the entirety of the island even during the periods of colonization under the Portuguese (beginning in 1505) and later under the Dutch (beginning in 1656). Rather, there were a number of fragmented Sinhalese Buddhist kingdoms scattered throughout the island, centered in Kotte in the southwest and in Kandy in the central highlands, and a predominantly Hindu Tamil Kingdom in the north of the island, centered in Jaffna. See Whall, 2000b.

[6] This history is in no way intended to be comprehensive. A multi-optic account is well beyond the scope of this analysis. For further details, the reader may consult a number of

Upon independence, Sri Lanka adopted a unitary constitutional structure. Many Tamil parties worried that this constitutional arrangement would not give minority communities protection against dominance by the majoritarian Sinhalese. By the mid-1950s, the parliamentary system (dominated by two nationalist parties and overwhelmingly representing Sinhalese interests) appeared unable to address Tamil needs and equities. Concurrent with the rise of ethnic Tamil concerns, a Sinhalese Buddhist revival gained newfound momentum and brought to the fore a number of policies that aimed to disadvantage the Tamil-speaking communities. Colombo pursued policies that were aimed at bolstering the relative position and strength of the Sinhalese majority throughout the 1970s. While interests in greater Tamil autonomy and even independence began to percolate in the 1950s and 1960s, the militant aspects did not fully begin to materialize until the late 1970s and early 1980s. As late as the 1970s there were still efforts to resolve the issue politically. In 1976, the Tamil United Liberation Front (TULF) was established. TULF subsequently won a landmark victory in the Tamil areas of the north and northeast in the general elections. TULF unsuccessfully tried to achieve Tamil independence through the parliamentary process.[7]

During the late 1970s and early 1980s, a coherent militarized Tamil insurgency that involved several insurgent organizations took form. These groups included the Tamil Eelam Liberation Organization (TELO), the People's Liberation Organization for Tamil Eelam (PLOTE), the Eelam Peoples' Revolutionary Liberation Front (EPRLF), and the Liberation Tigers of Tamil Eelam (LTTE). (The LTTE's commander, Velupillai Prabhakaran, founded the Tamil New Tigers in the mid-1970s, which later became the LTTE.[8]) The LTTE secured dominance among these groups through massive violence and coercion. While some groups still exist at various levels, the

---

sources, including Nesiah (2001), Asia Foundation (2001), De Silva (1999), Joshi (1996), Bose (1994), and Bush (1990).

[7] Ibid. and Kearney (1986).

[8] See Joshi (1996).

LTTE has established itself as the principal and most lethal voice of militant Tamil aspirations.[9]

To give some insight into the ethnic composition of Sri Lanka and the magnitude of the Tamil communities, Table 2.1 provides the most recent data for all communities. Due to the militancy in the Tamil-dominant areas, the last census that completely enumerated them was conducted in 1981. Although Sri Lanka conducted a census in 2001, the only Tamils that could be enumerated thoroughly were those who resided outside of the regions of the north and northeast.[10]

Table 2.1
Sri Lanka's Ethnic Composition

Ethnic Group	Population	Percentage
Sinhalese	10,979,568	73.95
Sri Lankan Tamil	1,886,864	12.71
Indian Tamil	818,656	5.51
Sri Lankan Moor	1,046,927	7.05
Burgher	39,374	0.27
Malay	46,963	0.32
Others	28,398	0.19
Total	14,846,750	100.00

SOURCE: *Sri Lanka Statistical Abstract,* Table 2.9: "Population by ethnic group and district, Census 1981, 2001." Available at http://www.statistics.gov.lk/abstract/population/tab0209.pdf. Note that no complete census has been conducted in the northern and eastern parts of Sri Lanka due to the insurgency. Therefore, data from the 2001 census does not include these high-density Tamil areas. Consequently, the values here rely upon data from the 1981 census. The Department of Census and Statistics, Sri Lanka, provides regional overall population estimates. However it does *not* estimate population for specific ethnic groups in those regions that were not surveyed.

---

[9] See United States Institute of Peace (2001), Whall (2000a, 2000b), and Joshi (1996).

[10] No enumeration was done in the Jaffna, Mullaitivu, and Kilinochchi districts. In Mannar, one in five was partially enumerated. In Vavuniya District, one district of four was enumerated completely and two were partially enumerated. In Batticaloa District, five of twelve divisions were enumerated completely and six were partially enumerated. In Trincomalee District, seven of eleven divisions were enumerated completely and two were partially enumerated. The data are not included for these districts due to incomplete enumeration. See "Sri Lanka Ethnicity—2001," available at http://www.rootsweb.com/ ~lkawgw/census2001-ethnic.html, last accessed June 27, 2003.

In the 1981 census, Indian Tamils comprised 5.5 percent of the overall population and Sri Lankan Tamils 12.7 percent. In the provisional 2001 results that excluded the Tamil-dominant areas, Sri Lankan Tamils were 4.1 percent and Indian Tamils 5.1 percent of the enumerated population.[11]

Background on the LTTE

Since numerous analysts have discussed the LTTE's operations and organization at length, here we will provide a brief sketch of the group, drawing out those features that are most salient to this analysis.[12] This section will also narrate some significant events in the rise of the LTTE, such as the arrival of the Indian Peacekeeping Force (IPKF) on July 29, 1987, and then it will describe the ascendancy of the LTTE and various elements of its global organizational structure.

The Indian Peacekeeping Force (July 29, 1987 to March 24, 1990)

Prabhakaran initially based LTTE operations in the mostly Tamil-populated Jaffna Peninsula and Jaffna City, where the organization's members operated as urban guerillas until the Indian Peacekeeping Force (IPKF) pushed them out. The best description of the IPKF operations to retake Jaffna is given by Lieutenant General Depinder Singh (2001) in the chapter "The Capture of Jaffna." Singh writes that the Indians made it their mission to capture Jaffna as soon as possible. He writes that

---

[11] See "Sri Lanka Ethnicity—2001," available at http://www.rootsweb.com/~lkawgw/census2001-ethnic.html, last accessed June 27, 2003.

[12] Again, the summary below of the LTTE is not intended to be exhaustive. Rather, it aims to give the reader enough background knowledge to appreciate the operational and tactical discussion of the LTTE given here and the concomitant state response. For further details, see Joshi (1996), *Jane's World Insurgency and Terrorism*, Vol. 15 (2002), Swamy (2002), Bandara (2002), Gunaratne (2001), Munasinghe (2000), Gunasekara (2001), and Balasingham (2001).

to a soldier, capture of a built up area is the most distasteful of operational tasks as it restricts the power of maneuver and entails house to house fighting which is not only time consuming but "eats up troops" and, inevitably, ends up in enormous loss to life both to the attacker and defender and the loss of life and property to the civilian population.[13]

Despite these reservations, the retake of Jaffna was important because it was the symbol of LTTE power and authority, one that had weathered all SLA attempts at capture. Moreover, the town was home to the LTTE's headquarters, training facilities, munitions factories, and caches of arms and ammunition. It was seen as a necessary first target "to bring the LTTE back into the mainstream."[14]

The IPKF actions in Sri Lanka are nearly universally recognized as a failure—even though they did manage to push the LTTE out of Jaffna. This is in part because the IPKF mission changed midstream: whereas New Delhi believed it was sending troops for peacekeeping, the IPKF became a combatant force countering the LTTE. Because the IPKF had not prepared for combat operations, it initially encountered enormous setbacks upon entering the peninsula. The force was grossly under strength. The units themselves were generally at 50 percent strength, and the number of units and formations were also inadequate given the task. LTTE tactics challenged the soldiers psychologically. The Indian soldier had never encountered an urban guerilla before despite India's vast experience with counterinsurgency in its northeast. The LTTE also made heavy use of human shields and blended into the surrounding population. Self-imposed Indian restrictions on the type of weaponry to be used in the civilian environment limited the amount of firepower that could be deployed. The LTTE also had superior weapons (AK-47s) and more effective communications systems. The IPKF was also handicapped by the order that it move along roads rather than travel cross-country.[15]

---

[13] D. Singh (2001, p. 90).

[14] Ibid.

[15] Ibid., pp. 113–115. Also see Fair (2003).

The IPKF observed a number of LTTE battlefield innovations. The LTTE cadres were always accompanied by an equal number of unarmed personnel. Their function was to provide extra ammunition and recover weaponry from their own fallen cadres and the IPKF, and it was their job to carry away the bodies of slain LTTE personnel. If they could not remove a corpse, they clothed the body in a *lungi* to create the impression that the slain person was a civilian.[16] (The lungi is a wraparound skirt-like garment worn by men in South Asia.)

The LTTE also made heavy use of improvised mines on tactically valuable roads to deter the initiatives of the 36 Infantry Division, which was tasked to keep the Trinconmalee Vavuniya–Elephant Pass road open. Elephant Pass was a key bottleneck that enabled safe passage of personnel, vehicles, and stores into Jaffna City from the port at Trinconmalee. The LTTE did not use anti-tank mines that would have destroyed the track of a tank, which would have taken some six to eight hours to repair. Rather, the LTTE burrowed holes under the road surface and inserted plastic cylinders filled with up to 100 kilos of high explosives. This technique would not disturb the blacktop and was difficult to detect. The LTTE used several types of activation devices, including pull and pressure switches that could be located at a desirable distance; electric current to complete the circuit; and remote control devices. This burrowing technique was so effective in its lethality and destructive capacity that IPKF personnel preferred walking to vehicle transportation.[17]

The IPKF did eventually succeed in taking Jaffna after two weeks of intense fighting and heavy losses. It did so by moving on the town through a series of coordinated thrusts that converged at Jaffna. However, the IPKF came under considerable criticism because it let the LTTE cadres escape into the jungles. Singh (2001) disagrees with these criticisms. He argues that it was impossible to isolate the town so effectively that no one could exfiltrate into the surrounding areas. Mustering adequate manpower for effective sealing operations was

---

[16] D. Singh (2001, pp. 107–109).

[17] Ibid., pp. 109–110.

likely inhibited by the fact that the Indian armed forces were recovering from or concurrently engaged in several military operations on the subcontinent.[18] The operations against Jaffna were also supported by operations in the Trinconmalee sector. 36 Infantry Division engaged in continuous cordon and search operations as well as raids and ambushes to ensure domination over the area. Control of this sector enabled the IPKF to keep adequate pressure on the LTTE to ensure that it could not get reinforcements to Jaffna.[19]

The LTTE quickly adapted into a highly effective guerilla organization operating in jungle terrain upon being ousted by the IPKF. Moreover, the experience gained from fighting what was then the world's fourth-largest conventional army enhanced the LTTE's effectiveness.[20] The IPKF withdrew from Jaffna after three years of struggle, and the LTTE quickly moved back to Jaffna City, retaining control of the city until 1995 when the SLA again pushed it out—albeit temporarily.[21] Over the two decades of its existence, the LTTE showed itself to be remarkably agile and capable of innovating and operating in both jungle and urban terrain.

The LTTE's Ascendancy

During April and May of 1986, as Tamil militants battled Sri Lankan security forces and Sinhalese militants, the LTTE founder, Prabhakaran, eliminated the rival group TELO by killing its leader and nearly all of its 300 cadres. By the end of 1986, the LTTE had fought several battles with the PLOTE and nearly eradicated the EPRLF.[22]

---

[18] The Indian armed forces were engaged in the Sikh insurgency from the early 1980s to early 1990s, as described later in this volume. In 1986, India launched an extensive military operation called "Operation Brasstacks," which Pakistan understood to be a mobilization for potential conflict. See Bajpai et al. (1995) for more details on this near-conflict. By the late 1980s, the Indian army was also increasingly involved in the Kashmir insurgency. For more details on the Kashmir insurgency, see Ganguly (1997) and Schofield (2000).

[19] Singh (2001, pp. 109–110).

[20] For details on the Indian Peacekeeping Force, see Bullion (1994), D. Singh (2001), and Gunaratna (1994). The Indian army is currently the world's second largest.

[21] Connor (2002).

[22] Ibid.

The LTTE effectively eliminated competitor organizations by the late 1980s and emerged as the preeminent military vehicle for Tamil aspirations. It had established a global organizational structure that few nonstate organizations can rival.

Today the LTTE is a preeminent militant organization that claims to be fighting for an independent Tamil state (Eelam) for the several-million-strong Tamil ethnic minority of Sri Lanka. (In 2002, the LTTE demonstrated its willingness to accept some form of autonomy within a federal Sri Lanka, an option that had previously been considered unacceptable.) Irrespective of the LTTE's ultimate objective of independence, in the near term the LTTE seeks to secure its hegemonic influence among the Tamil areas of the north and northeast by administering the apparatus of state. The LTTE has established a parastatal organization in the Tamil areas, replete with taxation, a judiciary, and security forces. This strategy permits it to obtain local financing for its operations and recruits for its military apparatus.[23]

LTTE Organization and Function

According to *Jane's World Insurgency and Terrorism* (2002), the LTTE is estimated to have some 15,000 cadres, with another 3,000–4,000 personnel associated with its naval arm, the Sea Tigers. (The LTTE has six ocean-going ships in its navy.) The organization is geographically structured and has seven regular commands. District commanders who ultimately report to Prabhakaran lead each command. The LTTE organization can roughly be described as "two-tier."

The first and dominant tier is the military wing that in many ways resembles a conventional professional army. The military tier has several specialized arms, including the above-noted naval arm (the Sea Tigers), a suicide force (the Black Tigers), and a highly specialized intelligence unit.[24] It is also believed that an airborne group (the Air

---

[23] See Joshi (1996) and *Jane's World Insurgency and Terrorism*, Vol. 15 (2002), available at www.janes.com.

[24] Chalk (2000).

Tigers) was in the planning process. (There is little evidence to indicate that it has actually been formed.) The second and subordinate tier is a political wing, comprising an office headed by a political leader, Thamil Chevlam. The political wing also includes the prominent political advisor and ideologue Anton Balasingham, who has been the public face of the current peace process.[25] Personnel of the seven commands are assigned to political or combat wings with further functional subdivisions.[26]

The LTTE also has a women's wing with an active, highly visible recruitment campaign. In the LTTE's 2000 offensive to retake the Jaffna Peninsula, the LTTE engaged the SLA with about 7,000 light infantry cadre. Of this figure, it is estimated that 3,000 were women. This proportion attests to the importance of women combatants in LTTE operations. Women are believed to be more effective in some roles, such as suicide bombers.[27] The Tigers effectively employ "gender manipulation": It is not uncommon to employ teams of three, made up of one female and two males. It is believed that this configuration motivates men to fight for the admiration of the female, who in turn is a highly competent and effective combatant.[28]

Once one enters the Tiger-controlled portion of Sri Lanka and travels by the Kandy-Jaffna road toward Jaffna City, he or she encounters numerous recruitment posters targeting women. These posters are intended both to encourage families to overcome traditional resistance to sending daughters into combat and to give a public face to the LTTE's platform of gender equality to all those entering the

---

[25] Chalk (2000). For more details on the military organization of the LTTE, see Connor (2002), DeSilva (1998), Munsinghe (2000); Swamy (2002), and Bandara (2002).

[26] *Jane's World Insurgency and Terrorism*, Vol. 15 (2002), available at www.janes.com.

[27] Connor (2002).

[28] Based on conversations with Bruce Hoffman regarding his January 2003 trip to Sri Lanka. This notion of incitement is a well-known rhetorical and literary device that has a long tradition in the Indian subcontinent. The taunt is usually a suggestion or direct accusation that a man is engaging in uncourageous and therefore unmanly behavior, and it implies either that women can be more courageous or that the men themselves have been feminized. For a fuller exposition of this notion, see Fenech (1995).

Figure 2.2
Photo of a Billboard "Welcome to Tamil Eelam"

RAND *MG210-2*

SOURCE: Photograph taken by C. Christine Fair.

areas under Tamil control. However, these posters are also intended
to incite men to join the LTTE. By depicting female valor and sacrifice, men who cannot meet the bravery of these female recruits are
feminized and demeaned.[29] Three typical recruitment posters that
line the road to Jaffna appear below. Figure 2.2 shows the first sight
one sees upon entering Tamil-controlled areas in the north: a unit of

---

[29] Based upon the author's visit to the Jaffna Peninsula in November 2002 as well as conversations with U.S. Embassy analysts, Sri Lankan police, and military officials.

women welcoming the visitor to "liberated" areas of Tamil Eelam. The second (Figure 2.3) depicts female LTTE cadres from the various wings of military operations. Finally, the third depicts a female cadre fighting the Sri Lankan army with lethal effectiveness (Figure 2.4).

Unlike conventional militaries, responsibility and promotion occur according to performance—not seniority. Moreover, cadres are not promoted to a "rank." Rather, they are promoted to increasing command responsibilities. Upon death, cadres are ranked using a system that reflects both their service as well as the circumstances of death. The Tigers make use of a number of prisons as well as torture and execution programs to ensure compliance among its cadres and to discourage dissent or abandonment of the organization.[30]

Figure 2.3
Depiction of Female LTTE Cadres from the Different Armed Wings

RAND MG210-3
SOURCE: Photograph taken by C. Christine Fair.

---

[30] See Joshi (1996); *Jane's World Insurgency and Terrorism*, Vol. 15 (2002), available at www.janes.com; Munasinghe (2000); Swamy (2002); and Bandara (2002).

Figure 2.4
Female Cadre Decimating SLA Forces

SOURCE: Photograph taken by C. Christine Fair.

The LTTE maritime organization is the most "formidable, non-state 'navy' in the world" and is divided into two distinct wings.[31] One wing is the "Sea Tigers," an amphibious group with some 3,000–4,000 cadres. The Sea Tigers are capable of operating in lagoons, territorial as well as international waters. The second maritime wing is a merchant marine organization comprising a fleet of LTTE-owned and -operated ocean-faring merchant vessels. The merchant assets operate independently of Sea Tiger command. Whereas the Sea Tigers are used to carry out terrorism (including maritime suicide attacks) and piracy, the merchant fleet is utilized for illegal trafficking of weapons, persons, and drugs. The Sea Tigers group has an extensive organizational structure, described in *Jane's World Insurgency and Terrorism*.[32] In addition, there is a female naval unit, and some 30

---

[31] *Jane's World Insurgency and Terrorism*, Vol. 15 (2002), available at www.janes.com.

[32] For more information on the LTTE naval operations and command structure, see *Jane's World Insurgency and Terrorism*, Vol. 15 (2002), available at www.janes.com.

percent of the Sea Tigers is female. There is also a naval intelligence cell that falls under LTTE military intelligence leadership. The dedicated suicide force, the Black Tiger organization, works closely with the navy.

There is comparably less information available about the putative "Air Tigers." The ostensible air wing leader, Vythilingam Sornalingam (a.k.a. Colonel Shankar), was a former Air Canada employee who specialized in suicide bombing instruction using microlight aircraft. Shankar was also educated in aeronautical engineering and flight schools in Canada. On September 26, 2001, Shankar was killed by a claymore mine. Reportedly, Prabhakaran supported the efforts of Shankar and bought several microlight aircraft to train the Air Tiger wing. Air Tiger operations were to be airborne suicide attacks, with cadres flying microlight aircraft filled with explosives into targeted buildings.[33] There is some dispute as to how far the LTTE progressed with its Air Tiger wing. Bandara (2002) claims that it did not fully develop this air capability despite the acquisition of aircraft and the LTTE's efforts to train operatives. LTTE cadres trained in France as well as the United Kingdom for Air Tiger operations.[34] There were unconfirmed reports of similar training in Switzerland and Australia.[35] However, this author could find no substantive evidence that this wing has ever been operational.

The Black Tigers are an elite arm of the LTTE that is raised exclusively for suicide attacks, the cadres of which are drawn from the best and most capable of the LTTE combatants. Black Tiger suicide cadres are fully integrated both into the LTTE's land and maritime fighting forces. The execution of suicide missions—nearly all of which are successful—has been the primary means through which the LTTE has been able to intimidate and coerce the government and the island's civilian (Tamil and non-Tamil) populations. The Black Ti-

---

[33] Jayawardhana (2001).

[34] Bandara (2002), pp. 526–527.

[35] *Jane's World Insurgency and Terrorism*, Vol. 15 (2002), available at www.janes.com. "Liberation Tigers of Tamil Eelam (LTTE) [Tamil Tigers]," May 22, 2002, available at www.janes.com, last accessed September 14, 2003.

gers and their operations will be discussed at length later in this chapter.

Consonant with the LTTE's parastate function, the LTTE Supreme Leader, Velupillai Prabhakaran, heads the Central Governing Committee. The committee is the body that oversees both the military and political tiers of the organization.[36] Within the Central Governing Committee is an International Secretariat headed by V. Manoharan. This body is tasked with efficiently and effectively maintaining the extensive and multifaceted LTTE transnational network.[37]

The LTTE also makes use of "outsourcing" to complement its formal structure. U.S. Embassy officials in Colombo explained how the LTTE is able to use contractors to obtain fresh and innovative ideas without compromising the safety of the larger operations. One of the examples this analyst provided is the exploitation of Tamil students within Sri Lanka's universities. Specific individuals within the LTTE are tasked with perusing the theses of Tamil students in programs such as engineering. The most promising students are selected and approached to be LTTE subcontractors. Such subcontractors will be tasked to design one component of a larger system. For example, the LTTE handler may explain to the student that the LTTE would like a suicide vest with a greater lethality radius. The student would be charged with devising one element of this system, for example the charge pack. Students so approached by the LTTE may comply either out of fear of reprisal against himself or his family or out of willing support for the LTTE's efforts. It is understood that once the task is complete, the student will have no further obligation to the LTTE.[38]

LTTE: A Global Operator

One of the most notorious features of the LTTE is the global scale on which it operates. Since the early 1980s, the LTTE has established a

---

[36] Chalk (2000).

[37] Ibid.

[38] Interviews in the U.S. Embassy in Colombo in November 2002.

global network of offices and cells that spans at least 40 countries and is unrivaled by any other insurgent organization worldwide.[39] Its global infrastructure serves numerous purposes. For instance, LTTE leaders operating in Europe have leveraged the Tamil diaspora to raise funds. In fact, some 80 percent of the LTTE's $82 million annual income comes from such fundraising.[40] In countries where the LTTE has been outlawed, it has operated under such organizations as the United Tamil Organization, the World Tamil Movement, and the Tamil Rehabilitation Organization.[41]

The LTTE has been adept at mobilizing the massive Sri Lankan Tamil diaspora as the "economic backbone of the militant campaign" through coerced and willing contributions.[42] In addition to donations from sympathizers, the LTTE also generates income by acting as a "proxy lender" whereby it puts up the initial investment in Tamil-run small businesses and the profits are split between the LTTE and the ostensible owner. These revenue streams are impressive: In Switzerland they are thought to raise some US $650,000 per month; in Canada they are thought to bring in C $1,000,000 per month; in the United Kingdom they raise an estimated US $385,000 monthly. The LTTE has other revenue sources, including gem trade and possibly narcotics traffic.[43] The LTTE also leverages legitimate economic activity among its extensive and sophisticated diaspora. For example, the LTTE invests in stocks, money markets, and real estate. It also owns numerous restaurants and shops throughout the world and has invested in farms, finance companies, and other ventures that have

---

[39] Gunaratna (1998). Chalk (2000) claims that the LTTE had cells in at least 54 countries as of winter 1999.

[40] Gunaratna (2000a). There are several such organizations. For example, see Byman et al. (2001); *Jane's World Insurgency and Terrorism*, Vol. 15 (2002), available at www.janes.com; and Le Billon et al. (2002).

[41] Ibid.

[42] See Joshi (1996), Le Billon et al. (2002), and *Jane's World Insurgency and Terrorism*, Vol. 15 (2002), available at www.janes.com.

[43] Davis (1996a).

had high profit margins.[44] Such financial maneuvering is advantageous because it is difficult to track and prosecute.[45]

Another major source of funding comes from the countries where there are large Tamil diasporan communities: Switzerland, Canada, Australia, the United Kingdom, the United States, and the Scandinavian countries.[46] Sometimes funds are given willingly out of the belief that the efforts of the LTTE are the only way to achieve autonomy and security for the Sri Lankan Tamil diaspora. In the United States, there are key wealthy Tamils who had given extensively to the LTTE prior to the organization's designation by the United States as a Foreign Terrorist Organization (FTO). One individual in particular, a California-based physician, has given as much as $100,000 at a time and is considered to be a "god" in the LTTE because he gives whatever they request.[47] In other cases, "donations" are collected like a tax by force or the threat of force, or through the exploitation of individuals who may be in a given country illegally and are seeking protection or assistance from the LTTE.

In addition to direct donations (coerced or willing) from the diasporan populations, the LTTE also exploits nonprofit organizations that allegedly provide social, medical, and rehabilitation assistance in Sri Lanka. The LTTE can deftly siphon funds from such organizations—or even establish front organizations to raise funds—because of the difficulty in establishing proof that such improprieties are occurring.[48] Whether or not the LTTE funds itself through narcotics trafficking has been hotly debated in recent years. In March 2001, both the U.S. Department of State and Sri Lanka's Narcotics Bureau denied having any evidence that the LTTE was funding its activities

---

[44] Gunaratna (1998).

[45] Le Billon et al. (2002).

[46] Chalk (2000); Fitzgerald (2003); *Jane's World Insurgency and Terrorism*, Vol. 15 (2002), available at www.janes.com.

[47] Chalk (2000).

[48] Ibid.

through narcotics.[49] But in May 2003 the Intelligence Chief of the U.S. Drug Enforcement Administration (DEA), Steven W. Casteel, contradicted this earlier assertion. Casteel testified that according to DEA intelligence, the LTTE does in fact finance its insurgent activities through drug trafficking. He further elaborated that "Information obtained since the mid-1980s indicates that some Tamil Tiger communities in Europe are also involved in narcotics smuggling, having historically served as drug couriers moving narcotics into Europe."[50]

The LTTE uses its global infrastructure to develop and maintain political and diplomatic support within host countries. LTTE lobbying efforts were tremendously successful in cultivating state support for their movements in world capitals during the 1980s and 1990s. Until recently the LTTE was able to develop political sympathy for its cause by mobilizing media and "grass-roots" and other political organizations over the issue of Tamil rights and the abuse of those rights by the Sri Lankan government. The LTTE effectively coordinates these efforts through a number of "umbrella organizations" established in key countries:

- The Australasian Federation of Tamil Associations
- The Swiss Federation of Tamil Associations
- The French Federation of Tamil Associations
- The Federation of Associations of Canadian Tamils
- The Illankai Tamil Sangam (based in the United States)
- The Tamil Coordinating Committee in Norway
- The International Federation of Tamils (in the United Kingdom)[51]

This extensive diaspora network is one of the most fascinating features of the LTTE. Apart from its utility in raising funds and gen-

---

[49] See India Express (2001).

[50] "International Law Enforcement Cooperation Fights Narcoterror: Drug Enforcement Agency Official Testifies Before Senate Committee," statement of Steven W. Casteel, DEA Intelligence Chief, May 20, 2003, available at http://usinfo.state.gov/topical/pol/terror/texts/03052004.htm, last accessed July 3, 2003.

[51] Chalk (2000).

erating political and diplomatic support, the Tamil diaspora has also expanded the LTTE's range of contacts for weapons procurement. Perhaps one of the most important aspects of the diaspora network is that it has brought the LTTE into closer contact with other insurgent groups. For example, the LTTE has established ideological, financial, and technological linkages with the various Khalistani-oriented Sikhs, the Kashmiri separatists, and other militant organizations.[52]

These groups, according to Gunaratna (1998), exchange and purchase arms from diverse sources that allow them to circumvent various international arms control conventions. The vast diasporan network has also allowed the LTTE and other groups to raise funds in one location, operate from another location, and fight in an altogether different place. This enables groups like the LTTE to exploit fissures among law enforcement authorities and the failure of government agencies to cooperate.[53] The Sri Lankan government has been helpless in the face of the expanding and increasingly effective LTTE diasporan network and has yet to develop means to vitiate the political and diplomatic strength of the organization's transnational backbone. Colombo has also not promulgated an effective media management strategy to counter that of the LTTE.[54]

The LTTE's Relationship with India

The northernmost tip of Jaffna is only 22 nautical miles from the Indian state of Tamil Nadu, and the journey takes about one hour by boat. As the name of Tamil Nadu suggests, ethnic Tamils predominantly populate this state. The LTTE saw this large and important population of co-ethnics to be an important source of support. The LTTE established links with a number of political groups in Tamil Nadu from the late 1970s onward. It managed to establish a few training camps in the southern Indian state without any official assistance from the central government of India by the mid-1980s.

---

[52] Gunaratna (1998).

[53] Ibid.

[54] See, *inter alia,* Byman et al. (2001), Gunaratna (1998), and Chalk (2000).

In 1983, Prime Minister Indira Gandhi made the decision to support the Tamil insurgency both for domestic (placating India's increasingly disgruntled Tamil population) and foreign policy considerations (stemming the increasing regional instability). India's external intelligence agency, the Research and Analysis Wing (RAW), executed this policy of supporting the LTTE. Within one year there were 32 training camps in Tamil Nadu, and some 20,000 Sri Lankan Tamil insurgents were receiving sanctuary, financial support, training, and weapons. These amenities were sometimes provided by the Indian central government, by the Tamil Nadu state government, or by the various insurgent groups themselves. Most of the initial training was conducted within Indian military and paramilitary camps in Uttar Pradesh. Some special instruction was provided through RAW at special centers in New Delhi, Bombay, and Vishakhapatnam. The most sensitive training took place at India's most prestigious military academy near Dehra Dun.[55]

India's policy of officially supporting the LTTE took a dramatic turn with the Indo-Lankan Accord of July 1987. India's abrupt policy shift resulted in part from New Delhi's realization that Tamil separatism in Sri Lanka could give a fillip to the separatist aspirations of India's own restless Tamil population. While attempts to placate this domestic constituency at first prompted India to adopt a policy of supporting Tamil groups, over time New Delhi questioned the wisdom of this approach. As a result of this accord, Prime Minister Rajiv Gandhi ordered the Indian Peacekeeping Force to go to Sri Lanka to implement a ceasefire agreement signed between the LTTE and the Sri Lankan army. However, the LTTE reneged and refused to surrender its weapons. The IPKF found itself fighting the LTTE rather than enforcing the peace. Indian army officers are critical of New Delhi's vacillating approach to the Tamil militants. The most authoritative account of the IPKF (Singh, 2001) notes that India's RAW was still training the Tamils *even while* the Indian army found itself fighting the same.

---

[55] Gunaratna (1998).

LTTE: Contacts and Training with Other Militant Organizations

Several Tamil groups received training from Al Fateh in the early years of the militancy, although the evidence is less clear on whether the LTTE specifically received such training.[56] The most important training that the LTTE received was from RAW.[57] There is evidence that in the 1990s several LTTE cadres were trained in Thailand by Norwegian naval instructors in underwater sabotage—a point that makes some Sri Lankans dubious of the Norwegian capacity to be a mediator in the current peace process. It is also believed that they obtained global positioning systems training in Sudan and political training since the mid-1990s from South Africa's African National Congress.[58]

The United States designated the LTTE as a Foreign Terrorist Organization (FTO) as early as 1997. Canada followed in 1999. Later in 2001, Britain and Australia similarly designated the group. It is believed that as a result of these designations, overseas Tamils have been discouraged from contributing to the LTTE. Interlocutors in Colombo also explained that diasporan Tamils who were coerced into giving donations were able to exploit the greater global enforcement

---

[56] Tamil cadres of the Eelam Revolutionary Organizers (EROS) traveled to Lebanon where they met with Abu Jihad (Yasser Arafat's military coordinator) and trained in the Al Fateh camp at Hamooriya. They trained for six months under a rigorous regimen that included physical training, the handling and use of weapons, and brief forays into the battlefields of Lebanon as a part of PLO patrols. Guerilla tactical training included survival courses, river crossing, swimming, traveling through sewers, and using rope to traverse obstacles. They became acquainted with a vast array of detonation techniques and weapon systems (e.g., pistols, revolvers, semi-automatic machine guns, AK series, M-16s, anti-aircraft guns, heavy machine guns, grenades, mines, booby traps, and explosives). Several Tamil militant groups sought training from the Palestinians. A group that subsequently broke away from EROS established ties with the Popular Front for the Liberation of Palestine (PFLP). PFLP training resembled the regimen provided by Al Fateh but also included ideological lessons. See Kulandaswamy (2000) and "Tamils Get Training" in Swamy (2002), pp. 93–114.

[57] TELO was the first group to be selected for Indian training, which promoted a competition between the LTTE and TELO. This competition honed the differences between the two. In a short time, nearly every functioning militant group had training facilities in India. See Kulandaswamy (2000) and "Tamils Get Training" in Swamy (2002), pp. 93–114.

[58] *Jane's World Insurgency and Terrorism*, Vol. 15 (2002), available at www.janes.com, and "Liberation Tigers of Tamil Eelam (LTTE) [Tamil Tigers]," May 22, 2002, available at www.janes.com, last accessed September 14, 2003.

and monitoring of anti-terrorism measures since September 11, 2001 to avoid paying the LTTE-imposed taxes. It is believed that these collective efforts have seriously retarded the LTTE's ability to raise revenue from its large Tamil diaspora in North America, Europe, and Asia. Moreover, the LTTE's ability to maintain its linkages with terrorist groups in the Middle East and elsewhere has also been seriously degraded.[59]

Suicide Bombing and the Black Tigers Cadres[60]

In some ways, the entire LTTE could arguably be declared a suicide force of sorts. Each cadre is required to wear a cyanide capsule, which is distributed by the local commando leader in the celebration that follows the completion of training. LTTE cadres have shown little hesitation in consuming the capsule if their mission is compromised. However, the most awe-inspiring arm of the organization is the elite dedicated suicide force, the Black Tigers (Karum Puligal in Tamil). The Black Tigers lead most LTTE military operations. A typical assault on a Sri Lankan army camp includes a suicide attack (e.g., a truck loaded with explosives driven into the camp). Before the army can recover, the regular cadres of the LTTE arrive to exploit the chaos and damage inflicted by the Black Tigers.[61] Notably, the Black Tigers almost always succeed in accomplishing their mission. President Chandrika Kumaratunga made history on December 18, 2000, when she survived a LTTE strike.[62]

As should be apparent, the Sri Lankan experience is invaluable to analysts of suicide terrorism. Arguably no other country has lost so

---

[59] See Byman et al. (2001); *Jane's World Insurgency and Terrorism*, Vol. 15 (2002), available at www.janes.com; and Center for Defense Information (2002).

[60] For the most extensive and comprehensive explication of LTTE suicide operations, see Kulandaswamy, Chapter 8: "Suicide Terrorism," 2000.

[61] See Chandran (2001); South Asia Terrorism Portal (N.D.); Center for Defense Information (2002); and International Policy Institute for Counter-Terrorism (2002).

[62] See Sambandan (2000).

many political figures to suicide terrorism in such a brief period. The LTTE is the only group that has successfully assassinated two heads of state, several presidential candidates (e.g., Gamini Dissanayake of the United National Party on the eve of the 1994 Sri Lankan election), and five cabinet ministers as well as numerous other political, governmental, military, and security force personnel. Moreover, the island nation's security, economic, and cultural infrastructure has repeatedly been attacked. For example, the Black Tigers effectively targeted the Joint Operations Command (the nerve center of the Sri Lankan security apparatus), the Central Bank of Sri Lanka, the Colombo World Trade Center, the Temple of the Tooth Relic,[63] and oil storage facilities in Kolonnawa.[64] Moreover, unlike many other organization suicide attacks, which have at least a veneer of religiosity, this is a *secular* phenomenon driven by a personality cult surrounding Prabhakaran himself.

Adoption and Innovation of the Suicide Attack

Sprinzak (2000) argues that Prabhakaran made a strategic decision to adopt the method of suicide attack after observing its lethal effectiveness in the 1983 suicide bombings of the U.S. and French barracks in Beirut.[65] The LTTE first began employing suicide operations in 1987 in its efforts to retard the movement of Sri Lankan troops into Jaffna City.[66] These attacks involved driving explosives-laden trucks into Sri Lankan army positions.[67]

The next innovation occurred in May 1991, when the LTTE used a female suicide bomber to assassinate Rajiv Gandhi at an elec-

---

[63] This is one of the most important Buddhist shrines in Sri Lanka. It is located in Kandy and has been repeatedly attacked by Tamil militants.

[64] There are numerous compilations of selected LTTE suicide attacks. See "Chronology of LTTE Suicide Attacks," (July 24, 2001); "Chronology of Suicide Bomb Attacks by Tamil Tigers in Sri Lanka (N.D.); and "Prominent Political Leaders Assassinated by the LTTE," (2001).

[65] Sprinzak (2000), p. 66.

[66] See South Asia Terrorism Portal (N.D.); Gunaratna (2000b).

[67] Connor (2002).

tion rally in India. This assassination was significant because it was the first use of a suicide body suit in South Asia.[68] Notably, at least one-third of the suicide bombers are women, and they have tended to be directed against political targets. One of the advantages of using women in this way is that they are less likely to be searched.[69]

Another significant development was the establishment of a naval suicide attack formation: the Sea Black Tigers. Prabhakaran adopted this tactic to counter the success of the Sri Lankan and Indian navies in denying sea-based supply routes to the LTTE. The Sea Black Tigers use small boats loaded with explosives to attack naval vessels.[70] According to interlocutors within the Sri Lankan Ministry of Defence, the Sea Black Tigers endeavor to use individuals who have been maimed (e.g., lost limbs, eyesight, mobility, etc.) in conflict who would not be effective in ground operations. This enables them to make the most of their available manpower.[71] It is worth considering whether or not the al Qaeda attack on the U.S.S. *Cole*, which used a small craft laden with explosives, exemplified al Qaeda observing and adapting LTTE sea-borne suicide tactics.

Gunaratna (2000c) notes six kinds of suicide improvised explosive devices (IEDs) that have been used in both South Asia and the Middle East: (1) human-borne (suicide bodysuit or vest), (2) vehicle-borne (car, truck), (3) motorcycle-borne, (4) naval craft–borne, (5) scuba delivery–borne, and (6) aerial-borne (microlight, glider, mini-helicopter). He explains that due to cost considerations, the most common IED is the human suicide suit and the least common is the airborne.[72] This author was able to confirm the use of five of these techniques. The author could find no instance of the LTTE actually using the airborne technique.[73] As noted above, the LTTE had

---

[68] Gunaratna (2000b).

[69] Gunaratna (2000c).

[70] Connor (2002).

[71] Interviews with officials in the Ministry of Defence in November 2002.

[72] Gunaratna (2000c).

[73] For an excellent inventory of Tamil Tiger suicide attacks, see Pape (2003).

planned to do so, but the Air Tigers have evidently fallen into disarray.

Globally, there are only a few other militant groups that have such a dedicated suicide squad, among them Hezbollah, Hamas, and the Kurdistan Workers' Party (PKK).[74] What is striking is the scale of Black Tiger operations: The LTTE executed 168 of the 271 known suicide attacks carried out by all groups throughout the world between 1980 and 2000 (see Figure 2.5).[75]

Classes of Targets

LTTE suicide attack objectives may also be categorized as human, infrastructure, and conventional military targets. There are generally two classes of human targets: national political and military leadership. Suicide attacks have been used very effectively against such high-value human targets. Civilian casualties are the result of attacks on such objectives, as civilians per se do not constitute a class of targets. The LTTE has yet to target leaders of the economic sector, in contrast to organized criminal and terrorist groups in India and Pakistan.[76]

The first high-level Sri Lankan political assassination occurred in 1991, when the LTTE assassinated the Sri Lankan defense minister, Ranjan Witeratne, in Colombo using a car-borne attacker. (This attack followed the assassination of Rajiv Gandhi.) Clancey Fernando, the chief of the Sri Lankan navy, was assassinated in a suicide-bomb attack in November 1992. In 1993, the LTTE assassinated Sri Lankan president Ranasinghe Premadasa by using a suicide attacker

---

[74] See Sambandan (2000).

[75] There are a number of tabulations that vary in some respects. Kulandaswamy (2000, p. 193) claims that the LTTE executed 180 operations between 1987 and 2000. Schweitzer (2000) maintains that from the early 1980s up to 2000, there were some 274 suicide attacks, of which the LTTE committed 168. Gunaratna (2000c) includes different groups than Schweitzer and determined that the LTTE conducted 168 suicide attacks between 1980 and 2000.

[76] See Kulandaswamy (2000).

Figure 2.5
Suicide Attacks Carried Out by Various Groups (1980–2000)

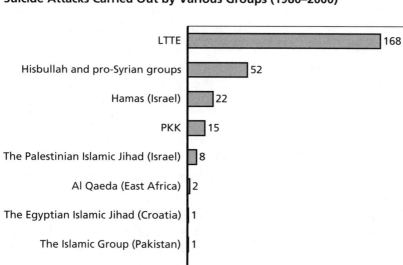

SOURCE: Gunaratna (2000c).

on a bicycle during a May Day rally in Colombo.[77] In general, the targeting of VIPs has tended to take place in the important urbanized areas of Colombo and Jaffna. In Colombo, the LTTE has targeted officials within the Sri Lankan government and security forces. In Jaffna, it has directed its operations against moderate Tamil politicians or rival organizations. Activities in that city are often aimed at coercing support from the local Tamil population.[78]

---

[77] See South Asia Terrorism Portal (N.D.); Gunaratna (2000b).

[78] Connor (2002).

In many respects, action against VIP targets is the easiest to conduct and also provides additional targets of opportunity (surrounding civilians) if executed in public. Successful attacks of VIPs, with their security entourage, require penetrating the target society, community, or government to mount massive surveillance and reconnaissance of the target. Successful execution also requires considerable rehearsing in a safe zone. The LTTE will rehearse an assault several times using stages, dummies, animals, and the like to perfect the lethal radius of the device and to work out other details of the operation.[79] For example, there are logistical requirements such as arranging safe houses, transporting the bomber and device to the location, as well as ensuring access to the target.[80]

A second group of targets is made up of infrastructure assets—of either symbolic value or utility value. Targets of utility value include the World Trade Center in Colombo, the Colombo airport, the Central Reserve, and oil storage complexes. (The 2001 attack on the Colombo airport is described in detail below.) Symbolic targets include the attack on the Sacred Temple of the Tooth Relic.[81]

A third class includes conventional military targets. The LTTE has shown remarkable ability to employ suicide attacks against these targets. The organization has used them to destroy military and paramilitary assets such as army, navy, and air force camps. It has also targeted logistical resources such as vehicles at airfields (e.g., Palaly), as well as both anchored and mobile sea vessels in ports (including attacks on the Colombo port). Kulandaswamy (2000), and others interviewed in Colombo in November 2002, assert that these battlefield attacks have not generally affected the Sri Lankan public outside of the insurgency-afflicted northern areas. Such interlocutors attribute this to the fact that assaults have tended to occur in remote areas and

---

[79] In the Tamil film *The Terrorist* (available in the United States with English subtitles) there is such a rehearsal depicted with apparent fidelity. This film was released in December 2000 and was directed by Santosh Sivan.

[80] Kulandaswamy (2000). Many of these issues were also addressed during interviews with Sri Lankan officials and U.S. Embassy personnel in November 2002.

[81] Ibid.

were far removed from the population. Kulandaswamy also argued that there has been a peculiar complacence about the insurgency that has prevailed among the Sri Lankan polity.[82] Officials interviewed during fieldwork attributed this "complacence" to a sense of distance from the insurgency: the insurgency is happening "up there" in the north.

Audiences for the Attacks[83]

It is also useful to understand the audience for an attack as well as the type of target and the venue. In cases of targeting rival Tamil groups and moderate Tamil political figures, the audience is likely to be other militant Tamil groups and political personalities. When targeting the security forces, the proximate target may be a general officer, while the distal audience of the attack is likely to be the foot soldier. Such an assault aims to degrade the morale of the troops and retard the ability of the Sri Lankan armed forces to recruit cadres and officers. Conversations with personnel at the U.S. Embassy in Colombo indicate that the Sri Lankan army is indeed faced with a grave officer shortage.

In high-profile attacks, the general population of Sri Lanka is also an important audience. Such attacks are intended to instill confusion and a lack of confidence among the populace as to who is in control. This is particularly salient for the residents of the north who have been closest to the conflict. The Tigers' ostensible constituents, the Tamils (at home and abroad), are another important audience for their operations. LTTE actions are intended to bolster the confidence of Tamils in the potential success of their struggle, serve as a recruiting tool, and serve as a warning to potential defectors.[84]

Attacks on national targets (be they personnel, conventional military targets, or infrastructure) also remind non-Tamil Sri Lankans

---

[82] Ibid.

[83] This section draws from the most lucid description, provided by Kulandaswamy (2000).

[84] Connor (2002, p. 99) has a similar discussion, although my analysis differs from his in some respects.

of the struggle by imposing direct costs such as the disruption of commerce, political crackdowns, or the psychic cost of losing a national symbol. Assaults on targets in Colombo also serve to attract the attention of the international community due to the presence of the international press and the various diplomatic missions in the capital.

Strategic Implications of Suicide Attacks

What is striking about the LTTE hits is their quality and accuracy. To achieve these successes, the LTTE has exploited the policies of the central government. For example, during the 1989–90 and 1994–95 peace initiatives there was a relaxation of security. The LTTE seized the opportunity to infiltrate into the southern parts of the island, particularly Colombo. Black Tiger cadres and LTTE national intelligence operatives penetrated the "hostile area" and were able to gain access to both human and infrastructure targets.[85] The intelligence cadres had two tasks: (1) mount surveillance on targets and infiltrate the relevant establishments (e.g., military, police, political, or intelligence); and (2) cultivate agents (typically residents) of the hostile area and charge them with surveillance duties. Reconnaissance data were dispatched to LTTE intelligence headquarters, where it was employed in operational planning. The LTTE would verify these data through alternative sources if needed. These data were used to build models for training cadres.[86] This training aimed to increase the speed and stealth of the cadre and, one could argue, to "familiarize" the cadre with an action that would ultimately result in her or his own death if successful.[87]

Individuals interviewed in the Sri Lankan military and intelligence maintain that during the most recent peace initiative, the LTTE has continued these practices. It is establishing operational cells and conducting target reconnaissance without hindrance in areas where it was previously denied unfettered access, such as Colombo

---

[85] Kulandaswamy (2000).

[86] Ibid.

[87] For a dramatic depiction of the acclimatization process, see *The Terrorist*.

and other areas in the south. This has led some within the Sri Lankan government to express concern that should the talks break down, the LTTE could exploit this newfound access, particularly in Colombo where the LTTE has infiltrated with a number of suicide squads.[88]

Kulandaswamy (2000) observed that while the *tactical* usages and significance of the suicide attack may be apparent, the *strategic* utility of this tactic is less appreciated and analyzed. Sri Lanka's political and military leadership (and arguably analysts of terrorism more generally) have paid little attention to the strategic implications and have been unable to develop countermeasures for suicide attacks or mitigating the impacts.

First, the suicide squad is part of an asymmetric strategy to target the state. While the LTTE "conventional" ground forces are capable of holding operations in the north and northeast against the SLA, Prabhakaran knows that these forces cannot engage the Sri Lankan security forces in the south. However, the LTTE can very easily slip Black Tiger cadres into the thickly populated city of Colombo and attack virtually at will.

The second and perhaps most obvious strategic implication of these operations is that the Sri Lankan political elite avoid criticizing the LTTE to avoid being targeted. In fact, some politicians have reportedly even gone as far as to express sympathy with the organization. Similarly, military leaders attempt to maintain a low operational profile and go to great lengths to avoid being perceived as spearheading efforts to destroy the LTTE.

Third, these attacks and the terror that they inspire ensure that there are few "public heroes" who are willing to challenge the LTTE openly. Kulandaswamy elegantly articulates the strategic impact of suicide attacks:

> The suicide-attack threat softened the stand of the toughest of leaders; compromised the position even of hard-line organizations; and debilitated the public will that had all along and

---

[88] Conversations with senior officials in the Ministry of Defence Military Intelligence and with analysts and diplomats at the U.S. Embassy in Sri Lanka in November 2002.

firmly argued that the LTTE must be fought to the end. While eroding the nation's political fabric the suicide-attack threat sapped the courage of the political and military elite. In turn, it degraded the moral strength of the public to unite, rally, stand up and fight against an enemy organization seeking to destroy the Sri Lankan state.[89]

Not only do the attacks deter the various elements of the public from confronting the LTTE, they have even encouraged public figures to placate it. Kulandaswamy further observes that even the most well-guarded political and military leaders declined to label Prabhakaran a terrorist or the LTTE a terrorist organization.[90] This situation persisted until the events of 9/11 precipitated a global change toward such groups, which ultimately empowered the Sri Lankan authorities and civilians.

Mythology of the Hero

The Black Tigers—and the family members they leave behind—are highly revered, and their sacrifices are honored in an annual celebration, Maaveerar Thinam (Great Heroes' Day). (N.B.: This expression is often incorrectly translated as "Martyr's Day," which has prompted some analysts to suggest that the LTTE suicide attacks are religiously motivated.) Prabhakaran takes special and personal interest in Black Tiger cadres. For example, LTTE cadres aspire to meet with him, as he is known to make few public appearances. Black Tiger cadres have access to the leader, and Prabhakaran will host a final meal with Black Tiger cadres before they set out on their mission.

As mentioned above, women comprise an important source of personnel for the Black Tigers, making up at least a third of the cadres. (The PKK is the only other known organization that has its own female suicide wing.) This has both ideological value, as it allows the LTTE to advocate gender equality for Tamils (this can be seen in its

---

[89] Kulandaswamy (2000), pp. 194–195.

[90] Ibid., p. 194.

recruitment strategies), and operational advantages: women exploit the innocent guise of pregnancy to conceal their suicide vests.[91]

The Black Tigers also serve an important ideological function. Unlike many Tamil militant groups, which used Marxist or socialist frameworks to motivate their cadres, Prabhakaran long ago abandoned ideological orientation. Instead, the mythology and reverence attached to the sacrifice of the Black Tigers serve to motivate the cadres.[92] "The Black Tigers thus form the backbone of the LTTE which in turn eulogize the former and this overt glorification ensures the continuous inflow Black Tigers have."[93]

Countering the LTTE in Colombo and Jaffna

The LTTE considers Colombo to be its most prized theater of operation. Because the insurgency for the longest time was seen as happening only in the north, Sri Lankans generally understood it to affect the residents of the north and the Sri Lanka security forces. Assaults on Colombo enabled the LTTE to bring the insurgency to the mainland. Because Colombo is the capital, targeting this city inflicted costs upon the entire Sri Lankan polity. As one official in the Sri Lankan Ministry of Defence explained, "Attacking Colombo has rich dividends. It makes leaders question the value of countering the LTTE. A single blast in Colombo has more value psychologically than full-scale conflict in the north and northeast."[94] The LTTE executed several massive, high-profile assaults against targets in Colombo, including the Sri Lanka Central Bank in 1996 and the Colombo World Trade Center in 1997. However, the single-most

---

[91] See Chandran (2001); South Asia Terrorism Portal (N.D.); Center for Defense Information (2002); and International Policy Institute for Counter-Terrorism (N.D.).

[92] South Asia Terrorism Portal (N.D.).

[93] Chandran (2001).

[94] Conversations with a senior official in the Sri Lankan Ministry of Defence as well as with analysts in the U.S. Embassy in Colombo, November 2002.

damaging strike in Colombo was the July 2001 attack on Sri Lanka's only international airport.[95]

A highly placed official at the U.S. Embassy elaborated upon the value of hitting Colombo. He explained that the war had always been "invisible" to most Sri Lankans. The government had established a number of "shock absorbers" to ensure that the insurgency remained confined geographically and psychically. For example, the government provided free medical care with heavily subsidized medicines. The Sri Lankan government also heavily subsidized fuel and food and provided an extensive welfare system. This official argued that such social infrastructure insulated most of the residents outside of the north from the economic impacts of the insurgency.

The Sri Lankan government also took measures to address the needs of its security forces. Sri Lankan soldiers are well paid by developing world standards and receive excellent pensions and life insurance benefits. In addition, there had been heavy censorship of the press in the past—including of foreign broadcasts. For example, the government had the technical means to block any foreign broadcast that mentioned Sri Lanka. (This practice was eventually curtailed, as they were unable to hear cricket scores!) This interlocutor also noted that whenever he attended military briefings on the conflict, the war was always depicted as being "distant" and remote.

Kulandaswamy (2000) made a similar observation regarding the LTTE's successful assault to regain control of the Jaffna Peninsula in December 1999. One of the key victories was against the army headquarters in Vavuniya. Despite the mounting SLA casualties, "life in the south . . . was largely unaffected by the northern casualties. There was a clear distancing from the battlefield, not only in geographical terms but also in mental terms."[96] Even for politicians, academics, and peace activists, the casualties in the north involved "someone

---

[95] Conversations with a senior official in the Sri Lankan Ministry of Defence in Colombo, November 2002.

[96] Kulandaswamy (2000), p. 171.

else's war."[97] This view persisted despite another defeat of the SLA in Kilinochchi.

U.S. officials interviewed for this work were astonished by the Sri Lankan government's initial effort to downplay and even ignore the implications of the strike on the airport. One U.S. diplomat recalled that after the attack, the Sri Lankan government called an emergency meeting. He attended this meeting and expected that the attack of the airport would be discussed. He recalled that during this meeting no mention of the attack was made, and indeed relatively ordinary and mundane issues were addressed—even while the plumes of smoke from the airfield were visible from a window in the meeting room.

However, this remoteness quickly began to fray as international airlines pulled out of Colombo and as tour group operators left Sri Lanka. Christmas bookings were cancelled, which levied a heavy loss upon Colombo's coffers. The insurance premiums applied to planes and ships operating in Sri Lanka were inflated to $100,000 per vessel per port call, as Sri Lanka was considered a "war zone." Consequently, imports became sparse and prices increased dramatically.[98]

While the airport attack was the most devastating to date and a clarion call to the Sri Lankan government, there is evidence that the complacence over the insurgency had already begun to erode by late December 2000 and early 2001. The sharp increase in oil prices was sufficiently steep that the government could not maintain its subsidy. Second, the rupee came under pressure and the government allowed it to float, after which the value of the currency exchange rate sank from Rs 78 to Rs 100 per dollar within three days. The business community was awakened to these problems and was suddenly focused on the war.[99]

There has been at least one advantage of the indifference to the war of most Sri Lankans that has persisted throughout most of the

---

[97] Ibid., p. 172.

[98] Conversations with a senior U.S. diplomat in Colombo, November 2002.

[99] Ibid.

country. Namely, there has not been a significant backlash against minority communities in the southern parts of the island. This contrasted sharply with the situation in 1983, when anti-Tamil riots occurred throughout the country after the killing of 13 soldiers.

The Colombo Theater

The LTTE has infiltrated the Colombo district and has established numerous independently operating cells. The group regards its success in the city as bearing directly on the government's war efforts to combat it. One of the key objectives of the LTTE in operating in this theater is to "destabilize the very seat of the government by assassinating important political personages who provide strong leadership in the war against the LTTE."[100] Consequently, political personages are forced to lead highly restricted lives because of the constant threat they face.

Second and equally important is the impact that their successes have had on the people of Colombo as well as of Sri Lanka. The population, in light of LTTE success and state failure, has come to doubt the ability of the state to protect them. As a consequence, people have increasingly been less likely to volunteer information to the security forces. This in turn has stopped the flow of intelligence about terrorist cells. The result is a spiraling degradation in the security environment within the state, whereby the paucity of intelligence has retarded the state's ability to pre-empt the LTTE's actions, which in turn continues to erode the public's willingness to come forward with intelligence to thwart the LTTE.[101]

Merril Gunaratne, like Kulandaswamy, has also criticized the state because it has tended to interpret the absence of LTTE activity as an abatement of the threat. Gunaratne (2001) has observed that

---

[100] Gunaratne (2001, p. 56). Merril Gunaratne was the Director General of Intelligence and Security in the 1980s. In the 1990s, he served as Senior Deputy Inspector General of Police. He was appointed Defence Advisor to the Ministry of Defence in March 2002. See "Merril Appointed Defence Advisor," *The Island,* available at http://origin.island.lk/2002/03/16/news05.html, last accessed September 14, 2003.

[101] Gunaratne (2001), pp. 55–56.

the most consistent feature of LTTE operations is the "inconsistency they deliberately practice in executing strikes. It is extremely rare that they would conduct two operations within a short space of time."[102] After executing an attack, "they bide their time, disarm us [i.e., the Sri Lankan security forces] mentally, and induce us to become complacent and drop our guard. The more important the prey, the longer may be the wait."[103] Therefore, he warns, the Sri Lankan security forces should be particularly wary of periods of inactivity.

Gunaratne, in his extensive experience in the security forces, writes with great clarity on the challenges of fighting terrorism in Colombo. He observes that although fighting insurrection requires an integrated organization of security and intelligence agencies, in practice this rarely happens. The types of operations that the LTTE conducts in urban areas and elsewhere require specific investigative capabilities, intelligence-gathering assets, and forces capable of multifunctional operations such as conducting raids, ambushes, searches, arrests, and recoveries. Gunaratne also argues, for reasons that will be discussed below, that minimum enforcement measures should be established and enforced as well.[104]

Gunaratne maintains that there is a strong need for special groups to conduct "psychological operations" (PSYOP) as well as civil affairs (CA). Indeed, these are functions that exist in different agencies, but given that PSYOP and CA activities should ideally be joint, there is a need for multi-institutional cooperation and coordination. At a minimum, PSYOP and CA functions need to be cohesive and organizationally integrated to effectively plan and execute missions.[105]

Gunaratne recognizes that each organ of state has its own administrative apparatus and that there are institutional impediments to cross-agency cooperation. Therefore, the task of ensuring cross-agency interoperability needs to be directed by a central commander

---

[102] Ibid., pp. 56–57.

[103] Ibid., p. 57.

[104] Ibid.

[105] Ibid.

whose job it would be to ensure unity in efforts and who would be responsible for the success or failure of his or her organization to meet objectives. This organizational approach is in stark contrast to the extant system in Sri Lanka, which instead requires the various security and intelligence components to work in a loose-knit liaison. Gunaratne, familiar with the work of Kitson and McCuen, cites the latter's insights on low-intensity operations that require "uniform planning, centralized control, and a single point of responsibility" as the basic minimum required to defeat a unified revolutionary movement.[106]

Gunaratne, reflecting upon this concept of "unified effort" vis-à-vis the police organization of the Range of the Deputy Inspector General Colombo,[107] notes that currently there is no such integrated system for counterterrorism organizations. Rather, there is an "ad hoc" quality to the cooperative efforts across the organizations, with specific counterterrorism operators being accountable only to the heads of their particular organization rather than to a unified commander who represents the apex of the counterterrorism activity.

The Deputy Inspector General in each Range is considered the "apex" of the counterterrorism effort in the current organizational structure. Gunaratne argues that this is an unreasonable expectation given the numerous other police-related responsibilities. There are also significant problems in getting intelligence to flow from central state intelligence-collection agencies and military intelligence to the police officers who are in "the boots on the ground."[108]

Perhaps the most crippling intelligence problem is that there are numerous intelligence organizations that do not operate in concert with each other. The premier intelligence agency is the Directorate of

---

[106] Ibid., p. 59, citing John McCuen, cited in Frank Kitson (1991).

[107] Under the office of the Inspector General (IG) of the Police, there are territorial and functional commands as well as criminal investigations and police narcotics divisions. The IG is divided into three geographic commands, known as Ranges, that cover the northern, central, and southern sectors of the island. See Jane's Sentinel and Security Assessment, Security and Foreign Forces: Sri Lanka, May 7, 2003, available at www.janes.com, last accessed August 31, 2003.

[108] Gunaratne (2001). This is also based on interviews with security managers in Sri Lanka in November 2002.

Internal Intelligence (DII), which reportedly suffers from understaffing. The police have an intelligence unit called the Special Branch (SB) that is also understaffed and underfunded and lacks the material and technical resources required to mount effective intelligence operations. Despite the manifold funding and manning deficiencies of these organizations, the central government also established an organization devoted to counterespionage. This, in Gunaratne's view, was ill advised. There should have been a consolidation of extant institutions rather than further diffusing material, financial, and manpower resources across a new organization.[109]

At present, the SB is required to support and augment DII activities. However, SB officers do not have the training, experience, equipment, technical resources, and funds to meaningfully contribute in this way. This is very unfortunate because it is the police who in principle could have the most specialized local knowledge, given their familiarity with the terrain in their area of responsibility. Under current circumstances, Gunaratne is dubious that the SB can operate effectively and contribute to the counterterrorism efforts of the state.

Militants operating in Colombo require a significant amount of logistical support and resources. First, they must be able to travel to Colombo and identify their safe houses. These safe houses serve as residences for the operatives, storage facilities for arms and explosives, and a location for conducting meetings and discussions. In addition, they need to establish secure modes of communication and execute undetected surveillance and reconnaissance of prospective targets to gather adequate intelligence to execute an attack. Necessarily, all of these processes require time and patience. The LTTE, despite its lethal effectiveness, cannot simply come to Colombo and carry out an attack overnight. It is during this period of time-consuming intelligence gathering, preparation, and planning that ample opportunities should be available to intelligence agencies to develop sources of information and arrest suspects.[110]

---

[109] Gunaratne (2001).

[110] Ibid.

While *prima facie* this may appear somewhat straightforward, in fact it is anything but simple. The intelligence leads that do come in are often vague and inadequate for action. Preempting terrorist activity is desired in principle, but it is impossible to thwart all attacks. Investigative capabilities are critical to the identification of culprits, means, resources, and supporting persons and material required to execute the attack. Postmortems on attacks are also an important tool for investigators to understand why intelligence was either not gathered or how vague leads could have been better interpreted or pursued. In Sri Lanka, such investigations are hampered by the lack of forensics laboratories and by the police force's rudimentary investigative skills.[111] The opportunities and requirements for intelligence gathering are illustrated by two cases detailing the LTTE's ability to infiltrate and conduct reconnaissance of the desired target: The 1993 assassination of President Premadasa, and the 2001 attack on the Colombo International Airport.

The assassination of Premadasa illustrates both the efficiency of LTTE operations and the inadequacies of the Sri Lankan security and intelligence apparatus. In this case, the LTTE planted its cell, including the suicide killer Babu, in the vicinity of the president's private residence. While the exact date that Babu moved into this residence is not known, it is thought that the LTTE took advantage of the then-ongoing peace talks with the government. Babu befriended the servants of the president, including the chief valet and even his protection officers.

Another example is afforded by the LTTE attack on the Colombo International Airport. In this attack, the LTTE destroyed eight Sri Lankan air force aircraft (including two Israeli-made Kfir fighters) and three civilian aircraft and damaged five more civilian planes. Eight men from the Sri Lankan air force and four from the army were killed in the attack. The LTTE was able to target both civilian and military assets in part because the military and civilian air-

---

[111] Interviews with U.S. Embassy personnel in Colombo in November 2002.

ports share perimeters in Colombo as they do in many other countries.

According to a well-placed diplomat in the U.S. Embassy in Colombo, the LTTE began conducting reconnaissance of the airfield by posing as street vendors who were picnicking in the park near the airfield. Several people observed these persons, and some individuals reported their suspicions to the police. The Tamils claimed that they were vendors. This provided cover for the various packages containing weapons that they were unloading and burying. The security forces questioned the Tamils and the reason for their proximity to the airfield but were convinced by their cover. As the Tamils were there for weeks engaging in the same activities, people ceased being suspicious. It is probably useful to point out that in South Asia it is not uncommon to find persons sitting on the ground selling various things with large packages of concealed goods around them.

In this way, they were able to observe the mandatory dark outs and the schedules of various military personnel accessing the base. They also noticed that many official personnel entered the base through holes in the fencing, which would later enable them to do the same without raising much suspicion. They first attacked the military part of the field. This interlocutor believes that they pursued the civilian side of the field only after they had successfully staged the military assault and saw that they could also attack the civilian side with ease. Oddly, there were no significant changes in the conduct of airfield security after the attack. In Sri Lanka, the notion of security is highly correlated with the presence of men with guns rather than enhanced security practices and procedures (e.g., enhanced airport perimeter defense, monitoring of entry and exiting of airfields, etc.). Indeed, there were men with guns for a while after the attack, but this has ceased.

The preparation required of the LTTE to carry out both the assassination and the airport attack provided, at least in theory, a number of opportunities to intercept and disrupt the cells. While it is not possible to intercept and disrupt every terrorist cell, Merril Gunaratne believed that there was considerable room for improvement. Gunaratne introduced a number of innovative structures to the Colombo police infrastructure targeted to enhance the ability of the state to detect, penetrate, and destroy suspected cells.

To enhance the ability of the security forces to obtain necessary intelligence, Gunaratne, as the Senior Deputy Inspector General (Ranges), introduced a scheme in Colombo to maintain "reasonable vigilance over virtually all households" in the various jurisdictions.[112] The city was divided into units of 75–100 houses, and the police established a vigilance committee (VC) among the householders in each unit. Two to three of these units were in turn aggregated to comprise a subsector. An officer with the rank of subinspector or a police sergeant was charged with responsibility for each subsector. It was his duty to interact with the VCs of the subsector, to notice activity that aroused suspicion, and to initiate inquiry either openly or through clandestine means of observation or surveillance. The basic principle of this arrangement was that this particular officer would become the expert on the persons of his subsector, cultivate informants, and note the arrival or departure of lodgers or tenants. In turn, several subsectors were further aggregated to sectors, under the authority of an inspector or subinspector. Several sectors would be grouped into a zone. The final consumer for the intelligence gathered through the system of VCs would be the DII.[113]

As should be apparent, this system requires a number of things to function effectively. First, it requires competent and professional police officers to oversee these decentralized units. It also requires that officers not be transferred. (Transferring personnel would forfeit the accumulated local intelligence and undercut the entire effort.) This system requires considerable resources in terms of manpower and material in addition to close supervision. It can quickly become ineffectual without all of these factors.[114] During the author's visit to Sri Lanka in November 2002, a senior official in the Ministry of Defence said that although the VCs were operating effectively at one point

---

[112] Gunaratne (2001), p. 63.

[113] Ibid.

[114] Ibid.

with all the required elements in place, they are no longer working well as a result of inattention to the critical factors.

Gunaratne observes that there were a number of problems even from the initiation of the VCs. The program was intended to produce informants and intelligence sources to further develop leads regarding suspicious residents and persons. This concept required that the policemen on hand be capable of collecting and developing this sort of intelligence. However, policemen were not trained in such counterterrorism operations and lacked the financial, technical, and other material resources necessary to perform effectively in this way. They were incapable of performing even the most basic operations, such as surveillance.[115]

The principal value added by the police officer is his ability to understand the local terrain. Even though the police are the right persons for the task, they currently lack the resources to work effectively. Conversely, the intelligence officers have the resources but are not in the right environment to reap the benefits of their resources. One Ministry of Defense official remarked with considerable vexation that in the current situation, intelligence collectors are "part-time workers" who face no threat because they are not "on the ground." This official quipped that these intelligence officers need to be in the hostile environment because that is where the intelligence needs to be collected. The same official further explained that the only way to overcome these hurdles is to have the intelligence officials and the military (especially military intelligence) act in concert with the police. While there had been efforts to achieve greater movement of information horizontally, all of these groups have a tendency to stovepipe intelligence through their own organizations.

The inability of the police to develop informants and useful intelligence leads has prompted the security forces to pursue options such as "cordon and search" operations. This sort of operation requires that every house in designated areas be searched thoroughly. Typically this would be executed in the early hours of the morning,

---

[115] Ibid., p. 64.

with the expectation that all residents would be home then. Another sort of operation is the use of pickets and roadblocks. These techniques inconvenience commuters, most of whom are Tamil. The Tamils have seen these tactics as humiliating. According to one high-ranking official in the Ministry of Defence, the Tamils have argued against both operations as being excessively intrusive. In his view these techniques have generated massive ill will among the Tamils of Colombo and elsewhere, most of whom are completely innocent.

These blunt instruments have proved counterproductive. They have alienated the Tamils and have provided fuel for LTTE assertions that Colombo is anti-Tamil. Moreover, in the view of the above-noted Ministry of Defence official, these actions have been so provocative that some Tamils may have become anti-state as a consequence. On this issue, Gunaratne writes that "One of the principles in counter terrorism is the need to avoid harassing the comity or racial, religious groups, whose perceived grievances militants espouse and exploit."[116] While there may be some limited need to conduct these sorts of operations, the cordon and search should be used only in highly limited ways and only on receipt of credible intelligence. Similarly, roadblocks and pickets should only be used on a "surprise basis" rather than a routine basis.

The other problem confronting the police in Colombo is that there is increasingly a blurring of distinctions between police and the military functions. Because the police lack the most fundamental and rudimentary counterterrorism skills, the military has increasingly become a domestic police force. To address this problem, Gunaratne suggested that the police force that may be most suitable for the Colombo environment is a special task force of police personnel who are trained for paramilitary operations.[117]

---

[116] Ibid., p. 70.

[117] Ibid., p. 67.

The Jaffna Theater

There is *symmetry* in targeting efforts and objectives shared by the LTTE and the SLA and Sri Lankan security forces. Whereas Colombo is the most highly prized theater for LTTE operations, Jaffna is also the most sought-after objective for the Sri Lankan security forces. Securing Jaffna is a "symbolic victory" for the security forces because of the salience of Jaffna City and the Jaffna Peninsula to the nationalist imagination of Tamils both within and outside of Sri Lanka. Denying the LTTE Jaffna also denies it an important source of bargaining power vis-à-vis Colombo. Moreover, sacrificing Jaffna or failing to secure it degrades the perception that Colombo can control the state and provide security for all of Sri Lanka's citizens.

Despite symmetrical objectives, there is clearly an *asymmetry* of burden and effort for the LTTE and the SLA to be seen as effective. The LTTE need only ensure that the SLA does not have full control over Jaffna to demonstrate Colombo's weakness. That the Tamil Tigers currently have tight control over the peninsula serves as a constant reminder to Colombo and to the citizens of Sri Lanka that the government cannot provide blanket security.[118]

If Colombo has failed to provide security in the capital, the LTTE's prized theater, its exertions in its prime theater, Jaffna, have not been effective either. In response to the 2000 LTTE initiative, it tightened an already stringent censorship that called for the banning of live broadcasts. In the resulting dearth of credible information about Jaffna and the rest of Sri Lanka, rumors spread quickly. One, for example, suggested that the LTTE specifically recruited young schoolgirls to pose as suicide bombers. In turn, police increased efforts to stop and check children at Tamil-dominated schools—which only furthered Tamil alienation.[119] Censorship was an issue of considerable debate. At first, a military officer was in charge of adjudicating whether a broadcast was suitable for the news. Later a civilian took on this charge. It was argued that in the absence of strict con-

---

[118] Kulandaswamy (2000).

[119] Ibid.

trol, the media would become a tool or a force multiplier of LTTE efforts. Arguably, however, the LTTE's sophisticated media-management apparatus thrived during this period, and in some ways it could be said that the Sri Lankans forfeited the information fight to the LTTE.[120]

In addition, Sri Lankans and the media have misinterpreted LTTE action much as the government has. The LTTE does not fight continuously: rather, it uses a "pause-and-pounce" strategy of intermittent assaults while resting in between. The Sri Lankan government interpreted the lulls in LTTE activities as signs of weakness or inability rather than a deliberate strategy. In what Kulandaswamy calls "a dangerous exercise of self-delusion, sections of the Colombo media projected the view that the LTTE 'wave' had ebbed. The pause-and-pounce pattern was seen as signifying the LTTE's decline."[121] Colombo miscalculated that the LTTE threat had passed. On May 10, 2000, the LTTE assailed the Kilali, Eluthumattuvaal, and Nagar Kovil defense lines. While these assaults were significant in and of themselves, they also served to distract the central government as the LTTE prepared for action around Jaffna City. The assault on the Jaffna environs led the way to the 2000 seizure of the entire peninsula, which was crowned by the seizure of Elephant Pass.[122]

There is evidence based on previous operations that the LTTE would probably have preferred longer pauses between assaults. However, Prabhakaran apparently felt that this was not possible for a number of reasons. First, to wrap up operations in the peninsula, the

---

[120] There are few cogent explanations for the failure of Colombo to develop a countering media strategy. Individuals interviewed in Sri Lanka offered only that Sri Lanka has not developed an effective media management strategy.

[121] Kulandaswamy (2000), pp. 117–118.

[122] According to Kulandaswamy (2000). In some respects, the LTTE was slower to consolidate its gains in the peninsula than would have been expected based on its performance in earlier campaigns. A number of factors appeared to slow the LTTE's advance, almost all of which can be attributed to logistical shortcomings. First, the LTTE had to move its cadres and arms in adequate end strength to the upper portions of the peninsula. Second, the LTTE had to build bunkers, pillboxes, and trenches at key vantage points. Third, timelines for moving artillery were lengthened due to the need to heavily camouflage the assets to protect them from aerial targeting and destruction.

LTTE would have to reach striking distance of the airfield and military complex at Palaly as soon as possible. The Palaly airfield is the farthest-north point on the peninsula and is the only means whereby Colombo can airlift supplies to its troops in the north. Bringing Palaly under a barrage of artillery fire would disrupt its supply line and greatly unnerve the SLA. Lengthy pauses would give the SLA time to regroup and reconstitute itself for fighting. Second, Sri Lanka was engaged in massive efforts to acquire arms and munitions. Prabhakaran wanted to finish operations there before the SLA could purchase, induct, and employ these new acquisitions. Third, and just as important, was the belief that the international community would step in sooner rather than later. Therefore it was essential for the LTTE to secure the peninsula to enhance its bargaining position vis-à-vis Colombo.[123]

The LTTE currently controls the Jaffna Peninsula as a result of the peace process. The LTTE has newfound responsibilities to the Tamils it now dominates because it claims to represent the aspirations of the island's Tamil populations. Therefore, it must provide effective governance and acknowledge the equities of the civilians now under its administration. In recent operations the LTTE has acted to protect civilian interests in its military operations. First, the LTTE understands that it must, to the greatest extent possible, protect Tamil civilians and their ability to earn a living and engage in commerce. For example, the LTTE does not put up bunkers in areas of commerce, wishing to avoid provoking Sri Lankan security forces to attack these centers of economic activity.[124] U.S. Embassy officials noted that this was in stark contrast to the operations initiated by the SLA, which frequently occur in commercial areas with untoward consequences for the residents as well as for popular opinion of the SLA.

A second consequence of this change in LTTE policy can be found in the efforts of the LTTE to retake the Jaffna Peninsula in the spring of 2000. (The SLA had taken back the peninsula from the

---

[123] Kulandaswamy (2000).

[124] Conversations with individuals in the U.S. Embassy, Colombo, in November 2002.

LTTE in 1995.) During the battle for Jaffna in 2000, the SLA had imposed a round-the-clock curfew on the town's 500,000 residents. The LTTE had made several widely heard broadcasts over its popular ratio station, the Voice of the Tigers, requesting Jaffna residents to vacate the town so that the SLA soldiers would not be able to use them as human shields.[125] Of course, another reading of these broadcasts would emphasize their utility in mobilizing the residents against the demonized SLA troops.

Third, in the LTTE's movements toward Chavakachcheri, it avoided taking the most direct route via the main Kandy road. (Chavakachcheri is the second-largest town on the Jaffna Peninsula and is about 15 kilometers east and slightly north of Jaffna. The map in Figure 2.6 gives details of this region.) Rather, the LTTE used a tactic of encirclement. This strategy permitted the LTTE to take the town while minimizing harm to civilians and civilian enterprises. This was a tactic employed by the LTTE in its more recent operations in Jaffna City. For example, the LTTE assiduously avoided fighting in the thickly populated areas of the city, choosing instead to encircle the municipal area. The LTTE's overwhelming concern has become civilians. It understands that causing immense civilian deaths would generate intense ill will among Tamils (at home and abroad) and within the international organizations and states upon whom the LTTE had depended before being proscribed as an FTO.

Another clear example of LTTE protection of civilian life can be found in its operation at Vavuniya. Before launching its assaults on the SLA headquarters in Vavuniya, the LTTE asked the civilians to leave the town in light of the impending attack. In response, civilians began leaving the area and shortly the entire town had emptied. Only those who could not afford to leave remained. (The author was unable to determine whether or not the LTTE subsidized this move with the provision of food, housing, and other support.) A few days later, the LTTE indicated that the civilians could return to the town

---

[125] Kulandaswamy (2000).

Figure 2.6
Map of Jaffna Peninsula

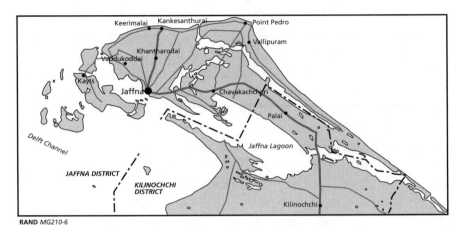

RAND *MG210-6*

but requested that they avoid any areas in proximity to the army camps, which was their planned area of operations.[126]

Lessons from Jaffna and Colombo

Both the analysis of LTTE actions in Jaffna and Colombo and a reading of the state's various responses suggest a number of persistent problems for the Sri Lankan government and its security forces. First, intelligence remains a problem. In addition to the resource and training issues elaborated upon above, another basic obstacle to intelligence is language. As a result of the Sinhala-only policy, very few persons in the state security apparatus have Tamil language skills. This is most problematic in the north and northeast. It is less of a problem in Colombo, but even there, Tamil capabilities are in scarce supply among the security forces—despite the large fraction of the Sri Lankan population that is Tamil and therefore Tamil speaking.

---

[126] Ibid.

Second, police officers are not equipped in any serious way for counterterrorism work even though they are in theory the operatives most well situated for such activities. An official in the U.S. Embassy in Colombo explained that the U.S. Federal Bureau of Investigation does provide in-country training. Due to resource constraints, however, the effectiveness of this training is questionable. For example, in the Ministry of Justice there is exactly *one* person who does forensic analysis. Moreover, when the United States does conduct training, it brings a number of sophisticated systems to use in the process. However, the U.S. teams depart with that equipment, which ensures that these programs have little efficacy, since the Sri Lankans do not have access to the technology used to train them.

In addition, the U.S. FBI does have some several dozen slots at the National Police Academy open to police personnel from various countries. However, some American and Sri Lankan interviewees suggested that the current programs are not geared for optimal results because of the process through which individuals are selected to attend the National Police Academy. At present, individuals are selected to attend for five months, after which they return to Sri Lanka. Cynical critics of the selection process suggest that it can be used to reward officers with a "vacation to the United States." In other cases, the process will send the "best policemen." At first blush, it makes sense to reward the best police officers with this training. However, it is probably optimal to send persons who are effective *instructors*. The best policeman may not be the best teacher and may be unable to disseminate valuable training acquired in the United States.

Third, Sri Lanka does not have clearly defined roles for its police and military. (India and Pakistan have adopted a different approach of using an intermediate force between the army and the police, comprised of a number of paramilitary organizations.) As a consequence, the army is consistently brought in for internal security duties while the police force continues to lack the basic skills and training that it needs to be effective. Although there is a case to be made that Sri Lanka has no significant external enemy and therefore this may not be an unreasonable duty for the army, there are untoward consequences of this approach. First and foremost, civilians are not likely to welcome an omnipresent military force. Second, the use of the army for police duties may impair the army's ability to recruit and retain officers. These implications for the army's end-strength are derived from the insights of the Ministry of Defence, which explained that the constant confrontation with the LTTE has resulted in these manpower-related problems and has even encouraged desertions among the troops.

Summary Analysis of the Impacts of 9/11 upon the LTTE

In December 2001, the LTTE initiated a unilateral ceasefire when the United National Front (UNF) government came to power. This resulted in a peace process that continues to date, albeit with a number of obstacles and with less momentum than it initially had. In some ways, the LTTE was militarily at the height of its power when it entered into a ceasefire. Through its attack on the international airport, it severely affected the Sri Lankan economy and brought the insurgency to the home of nearly every Sri Lankan via the extensive media coverage. Yet only a few months later the LTTE agreed to a ceasefire. What motivated this?

While the LTTE had demonstrated its ability to project power through force, the events of 9/11 brought a number of changes in the global and domestic environment that are illustrative for combating militant organizations like the LTTE. Although many states had taken efforts to proscribe the LTTE well before 9/11, interviewees in Colombo perceive the tragic events as having galvanized the international community to take the organization and its supporters more seriously and to adopt more rigorous monitoring and enforcement of anti-terrorism measures.

This changed global environment affected both coerced and willing LTTE contributors. Coerced contributors were emboldened to refuse to pay the "revolutionary tax" to the LTTE, citing the increased vigilance of the FBI or other domestic law enforcement agencies. Interlocutors in Colombo also believed that such individuals were more encouraged to report these activities, providing intelligence on local LTTE cells. For the willing supporters of the LTTE, the costs of contributing rose significantly. Many of these individuals are wealthy professionals and had much to lose if they were caught donating to a foreign terrorist organization.

According to interlocutors at the U.S. Embassy in Colombo, many overseas Tamils who supported the LTTE were dismayed at being cast as a terrorist group. Despite LTTE's insistence that it is an insurgent organization, the global community was no longer interested in entertaining such distinctions. Reportedly, diasporan Tamils sought out LTTE representatives and encouraged them to abandon the military struggle, pursue a diplomatic solution, and restore the image of the LTTE.

Some analysts observed that even before the events of 9/11, the diaspora had become increasingly "jittery" about the activities of the LTTE. For example, the forcible recruitment of children and the tactic of suicide bombing compelled some supporters to question the LTTE's operations.[127]

Thus, at one level, the events of 9/11 generated sufficient economic, political, and diplomatic pressure to push the LTTE to negotiate despite its tactical advantages on the battleground. However, another piece of the puzzle is that the LTTE actually gained substantially under the ceasefire.

First, the LTTE was able to recoup its lost credibility both because it was de-proscribed in Sri Lanka (although not elsewhere) and because it became a co-participant (with varying degrees of equality) in multilateral forums alongside the Sri Lankan government. (However, the LTTE's ample media-management assets certainly depicted it as an equal participant.) This restored the legitimacy that the LTTE craved in international circles and acted to restore the perception that it is in fact an insurgent organization.

Second, subsequent to the ceasefire the number of LTTE cadres has increased substantially—one estimate claimed that it might have

---

[127] Comments made by Neil DeVotta at "Sri Lanka: Prospects for Peace," a half-day seminar held at CSIS, February 14, 2003. Summarized in http://www.csis.org/pubs/Insights/03MarApr.pdf, last accessed September 16, 2004.

tripled.[128] This is because the LTTE publicized that it would offer preferential hiring to LTTE cadres in whatever interim parastate organization emerged from the ceasefire. This had the effect of increasing the *value* of LTTE participation. Simultaneously, the likelihood of confronting danger was minimized as a result of the ceasefire, thereby reducing the *cost* of LTTE membership.

Moreover, as a result of the ceasefire, the LTTE has been able to establish cells throughout the country with ease, while the Sri Lankan security apparatus, under the terms of the ceasefire, can do nothing to stop it. (It is surprising that Colombo agreed to these terms, as this appears to be the standard method that the LTTE uses to exploit peace processes.)

The incentive structure motivating the state's interest is also complex. On the one hand, Colombo could have chosen to exploit the changed international environment and launch a further military assault on the LTTE. It does appear that Colombo realizes that with its current assets and training, a military solution is not feasible. It is also likely that the attack on the Colombo airport demonstrated the LTTE's at-will ability to seriously affect Sri Lanka's economic health. This realization, in conjunction with a sober review of the SLA's present capabilities, may have motivated Colombo to exploit the changed strategic environment for the LTTE to pursue a diplomatic solution.

However, there were costs in doing so. Sri Lanka had to deproscribe the LTTE, and Colombo has had to tolerate the fact that in the short term the LTTE will benefit the most from the process. In the long term, however, Colombo could well come to reap the benefits. Despite 20 years of civil war, the Sri Lankan economy has fared reasonably well compared to other states in its neighborhood. Should the civil war be put to rest, Colombo can get on with the business of developing its economy.

---

[128] Conversations with senior officials in the Ministry of Defence in November 2002 in Colombo. Also see comments of Neil DeVotta, CSIS, February 14, 2003.

CHAPTER THREE

India

Preview of the Findings

This chapter takes as its subject the militancy waged by Sikh separatists seeking an independent state, Khalistan, to be carved out of the north Indian state of the Punjab. This chapter focuses explicitly on developments within the movement following the 1984 Indian army raid on the Sikhs' most sacred shrine: the Golden Temple. (This action was called Operation Bluestar.) Analysis of the post–Operation Bluestar militancy identified several innovations made by the Khalistani activists, which are detailed herein.

Following Operation Bluestar, the militancy morphed into a distinctively more urban phenomenon. Operation Bluestar, perceived by many as a mass insult to the Sikh community, precipitated widespread disaffection among the Sikhs. The militancy's urban movement was facilitated by the All India Sikh Students Federation and through the successful penetration of universities, which tended to be in urbanized areas. According to some Indian analysts of the militancy, the disaffection in the Punjab created a target of opportunity for Pakistan, which funneled resources into the movement to enhance its lethality and efficacy.

The movement to the urbanized areas created numerous opportunities for fundraising, which were almost exclusively criminal in nature and included kidnapping, extortion, and high-profile robberies. Urbanization facilitated criminalization by giving Khalistani activists the opportunity to network with organized crime syndicates.

(This contrasts with the LTTE, which used both legal and illegal revenue-raising means.)

Khalistani activists also took advantage of the legal "no man's land" that existed in those areas where many states are contiguous—such as the region surrounding New Delhi. Militants found that they could easily reside in one state, base their operations and logistics in another, and carry out attacks in New Delhi, for example. This strategy permitted the militants to exploit the lack of coordination and cooperation among the various state law enforcement and intelligence agencies as well as among the various state and central counterterrorism organizations.

Khalistani activists made a number of targeting innovations (e.g., the development and placement of IEDs, the use of remote and time-delayed detonation devices). It is believed by some that Khalistani activists may have learned some of these improvements by interacting with the LTTE. There is more credible evidence that they also received training from U.S.-based mercenary schools.

Eventually, the Indian security apparatus did manage to evolve adequate structures to counter the Khalistani separatists. The Indian security forces were at first hindered by undertrained and ill-equipped police forces that were not operating in an integrated fashion with the intelligence, military, and paramilitary outfits that were also involved in the counterinsurgency effort. Moreover, the use of *both* police and military forces created a number of problems, which are detailed herein. Over time, the Indian security forces learned to more effectively task specific security forces with elements of the militancy.

The Indian government also evolved relatively sophisticated interagency meetings that involved relevant institutions from the central government as well as all of the key states. This was an important development that allowed Indian security forces to deny militants use of the legal no man's land that they cultivated. The state police also found ways to improve their relations with the residents, which created means for gathering more effective intelligence leads. This generated a positive cycle: access to better information about the militants and their operations enabled the police to take more targeted action, enhanced their ability to protect citizens, and decreased arbitrary or indiscriminate action. This in turn continued the improvements in the police/policed relationship. For sure, it is not our argument that this relationship is currently unproblematic. It is probably safe to say that given the mandate of the police in India, a fully functional relationship between the police (widely seen as corrupt and ineffective) and the populace is not likely in the policy-relevant future.

The Indian government also began to appreciate the specific utility of the media in shaping public opinion about the Sikh militancy to degrade its support among Sikhs within India. The Indian security forces—learning from the debacle of Operation Bluestar—learned to search Sikh religious institutions with greater sensitivity toward the people. These operations were both intended to be (and explained to the community to be) preemptive in that they aimed to locate militants *before* they could take over a particular shrine as well as to deter them from pursuing this strategy in the future. The Indian security forces also relied heavily upon deception as a "force multiplier" to ameliorate the limitations imposed upon the security forces by lack of funds and other resources.

Introduction to the Case

India has been battling one form or another of low-intensity conflict virtually incessantly since it became independent in 1947. In the 1950s, India struggled with an insurgency it inherited from the British administration in the Naga Hills, in India's northeastern state. In the 1960s, insurgency spread to other areas of India's northeast, including Mizoram, Manipur, and Tripura. During the 1970s, conflict spread to Assam—also in India's northeast. Notably, these conflicts are still ongoing. As this part of the country is lush and verdurous, India has mostly waged its counterinsurgency campaigns in jungle terrain and in small villages. (Although some of this conflict in the northeast has certainly had urban or semiurban components.) However, the natural urbanization of India has meant that the state's encounters with such insurgent elements in the northeast are occurring in increasingly built-up areas.

In the 1980s, these events were completely overtaken by the low-intensity conflict waged in the troubled state of Punjab, where factions of Sikh separatists engaged in a sustained campaign of militant violence to secure an independent Sikh homeland, Khalistan. Since the political, social, and economic history of this movement has been well documented and debated, those aspects of the conflict will not be rehashed here.[1] There were several groups engaged in this struggle for an independent Khalistan, including the Khalistan Commando Force and the Babbar Khalsa.

This insurgent movement was exceptionally brutal and claimed the lives of over 21,000 persons before it was effectively eliminated by 1993. (In comparison, the terrorism in Northern Ireland claimed 1,686 lives between 1969 and 1976.) The insurgency in Punjab took more lives than the combined wars with Pakistan, in which 2,700 army personnel perished, yet this conflict has not drawn the attention of terrorism analysts.[2] There has been no tactical history written about the movement and the state's efforts to squash it. This case merits further study not only because of the movement's scope and lethality, but because it was one of the few insurgencies that has been systematically defeated. India's urban centers are targeted by a host of other criminal and militant organizations. In recent years, militants who are trained and based in Pakistan have conducted a number of significant operations in New Delhi. In 2000, Lashkar-e-Taiba (LeT) struck the Red Fort, an important tourist destination in that city.[3]

---

[1] See Goulbourne (1991); Kapur (1986); Axel (2001); Tully and Jacob, (1991); Brar (1993); Juergensmeyer (2000); Mahmood (1996); and Fox (1990).

[2] These data are from Gill (1999). There are several estimates of the death toll of this insurgency; this is simply one figure.

[3] There does appear to be some asymmetry in the ways in which the LeT and the Indian observers interpret the significance of that attack. The LeT claims that it targeted the Red Fort because part of the structure houses various military units and a high-security interrogation cell, used both by the Central Bureau of Interrogation and the army. (Conversation with a spokesperson of the LeT in August 2003.) In contrast to the LeT perception of the Red Fort's military significance, Indian press reports instead stress its figurative importance as a symbol of independent India. See "Militants Storm Red Fort in Delhi," Rediff on the Internet, December 22, 2000, available at http://www.rediff.com/news/2000/dec/22fort1.htm, last accessed September 10, 2003. See also Aneja (2000).

The Jaish-e-Muhammed, possibly acting in concert with the LeT, conducted a suicide attack on the Indian Parliament on December 13, 2001. That attack precipitated the largest mobilization of Indian troops since its 1971 war with Pakistan and kept the two countries at a near state of war for most of 2002.

The vast Indian experience with numerous terrorist and organized criminal organizations offers a wealth of lessons learned. The case that will comprise the primary focus of this chapter will be the Sikh insurgency in the Indian state of Punjab, the so-called Khalistan movement. We are focusing upon this insurgency in part because the Punjab insurgency represents a sustained campaign of violence that demonstrates the evolution of both the militancy and the response of security forces over time.

Although the recent attacks in New Delhi and elsewhere by Pakistan-backed militants offer interesting details about militant operations, it is harder to argue that they represent a sustained campaign of urban terrorism. This is a battle that is currently waged by the Indian security forces and is deeply tied to the ongoing security competition with Pakistan. Therefore it is difficult to find interlocutors who are willing to articulate the ways in which the security forces have evolved to deal with this new threat. This will comprise an important area for future inquiry as data become more available.

The Khalistan Movement[4]

The idea of Sikh separatism first arose in the early 20th century with the rise of Sikh nationalism in British India. This movement should be understood within the context of religious nationalist movements that were gaining traction in the same period. These religio-nationalist movements emerged in response to British "divide and rule" administrative policies; the perceived success of Christian mis-

---

[4] This history is not intended to be comprehensive. Additional sources are provided throughout. This is only intended to provide a thoroughly unfamiliar reader with some sense of the movement and its consequences.

sionaries converting Hindus, Sikhs, and Muslims; and a general belief that the solution to the downfall among India's religious communities was a grass roots religious revival. Hindus, Sikhs, and Muslims all experienced various degrees of religious revivalism. This process inherently involved differentiating the various communities and establishing communal boundaries.[5]

As the Muslim League began asserting the "Two Nation Theory" (which argued that Hindus and Muslims comprised different nations) to lay the groundwork for a separate Muslim state, Sikhs began to ponder their own fate. As independence from the British neared and two states appeared increasingly likely, Sikhs questioned how their interests would be protected in an overwhelmingly Hindu, albeit democratic, state. Many Sikhs believed that they should have been granted a separate state.[6] This sense of entitlement was bolstered by the extensive military service by the Sikhs in the Royal Indian Army during the world wars.[7]

Although the notion of a separate Sikh state had been around since the early 20th century, it was in the decades following Indian independence that the issue became more seriously pursued by its advocates. Strands of a Sikh nationalist struggle began to militarize in the 1970s and 1980s. Sant Jarnail Singh Bhindranwale emerged as a high-profile leader of the Sikh militancy in the early 1980s when he and his militant cadres took refuge in the Sikh's holiest shrine, the

---

[5] Kapur (1986), Oberoi (1988), Barrier (1988), A. Singh (1988), Axel (2001), and Mahmood (1996).

[6] The story of Sikh nationalism must be seen in the context of the concurrent Hindu nationalist project, which attempted to absorb Sikhs into the fold of Hinduism. Sikh nationalists rejected the Hindu nationalist claim that Sikhs are Hindus and sought to establish clear boundaries of identity through, *inter alia,* the development of new Sikh rituals (e.g., for birth, marriage, death, etc.) and the mobilization of the legal system to attain legitimacy for these new rituals (e.g., the Sikh Marriage Act). A thorough discussion of this phenomenon is well beyond the scope of this work. The salient point is that as a result of myriad religio-political identity movements in the subcontinent, a number of Sikh political entrepreneurs began formalizing the demand for Sikh sovereignty well before the 1980s. For comprehensive accounts of this complex and highly contested process, the reader should consult Kapur (1986) and Oberoi (1988, 1994).

[7] See, *inter alia,* Kapur (1986); Oberoi (1988); Barrier (1988); A. Singh (1988); Axel (2001); and Mahmood (1996).

Golden Temple, to avoid being arrested. Bhindranwale did not rise to prominence solely by his own efforts. Indira Gandhi explicitly chose to buttress his political following in an effort to split the Akali Dal (the most prominent Sikh political party in the Punjab), which was in opposition to her Congress party. In hindsight, this was a tremendous miscalculation, as Bhindranwale, with his separatist political objectives, gained popularity within segments of the Sikh population (e.g., the traditional agricultural caste, the *Jats*). His vociferous and militant position revealed the relatively moderate position taken by the Akali Dal.[8]

In June 1984, Indira Gandhi ordered the army into the Golden Temple complex to wrest it from the militants in an operation that was named "Operation Bluestar."[9] Bhindranwale perished in this operation, but the militancy was not crushed. Mrs. Gandhi's Sikh bodyguards assassinated her in revenge, after which thousands of Sikhs perished in Hindu attacks upon them and their communities throughout India. Operation Bluestar and the ensuing massacres of Sikhs fostered a wider-spread militancy among the Sikhs in the Punjab by legitimizing the separatists' claims that India could not and would not protect Sikh interests. Operation Bluestar and its bloody sequelae also galvanized the millions of diasporan Sikhs to espouse this cause.

The involvement of the diaspora was an important dimension of the Sikh insurgency. Not only was it a source of diplomatic and financial support, it was also a factor in enabling Pakistan to get involved in fueling the Sikh separatist efforts. Sikhs in Canada, the United Kingdom, and the United States played important roles in arranging for cadres to travel to Pakistan, where they received financial and military assistance. A number of Sikh groups in the diaspora

---

[8] In particular, many analysts within India and without contend that Giani Zail Singh (who eventually became the president of India in 1982) developed Bhindranwale as a foil to the Akali government to diminish the ability of the Akalis to challenge the electoral authority of the Congress party in Punjab. See Nayar and Singh (1984). For a more detailed account of this miscalculated strategy of Indira Gandhi's Congress party, see Tully and Jacob (1991), Telford (1992), Kapur (1986), Pettigrew (1995), and Malik (1986),

[9] For a comprehensive account of Operation Bluestar, see Brar (1993).

declared themselves to be the Khalistan government in exile following the attack on the Golden Temple.[10] There was a proliferation of Khalistani militant outfits throughout the 1980s and 1990s, including Babbar Khalsa, the Khalistan Commando Force, the Khalistan Liberation Force, the Bhindranwale Tiger Force of Khalistan, the Khalistan Liberation Organization, and the International Sikh Youth Federation. Many of these organizations are described in the following section.

Analysts of terrorism in South Asia have criticized the way in which the Sikh insurgency has been characterized in the academic literature. Ajai Sahni (2001), for example, writes that much of the literature on the conflict has been rife with inaccuracy, written from views that take the perspective of the Sikh insurgents at face value and deny the histories of the victims who were also predominantly Sikh.[11] That the academic literature has largely taken on the narrative of the insurgent movement attests to the success of an important strategy of the Sikh diaspora. Proponents of the Khalistan movement established strongholds in academic universities throughout North America and the United Kingdom by establishing Sikh studies chairs at major universities or creating soft money teaching positions for scholars of Sikhism and Punjabi language studies. Proponents of Khalistan have pursued academia to ensure control over the production of knowledge about their community and to shape the way students understand Sikhs, Sikhism, and their religio-political goals.[12] Sikh diasporan institutions have also been effective at cultivating diplomatic and ideological support through political action committees and organized direct action.[13]

---

[10] Shani (2002).

[11] Sahni (2001).

[12] O'Connell (1993). See also Mann (1993).

[13] For an example of the political support they have generated in the United States, see Congressional Record Statements available at http://www.khalistan.com, last accessed September 9, 2003. For an example of some of their activities in Canada, see "Dhaliwal lobbies to save jailed terrorist from hanging," April 7, 2003, available at http://www.ftlcomm.com/

Major Khalistani Organizations

In this section we provide information about the key militant groups that will be described in this case study. This inventory of militant groups is not intended to be comprehensive.

Babbar Khalsa

This organization came into prominence in 1981. Its members maintained a low level of activity until 1983. It drew its membership from ex-servicemen, policemen, and particular Sikh religious organizations. The organization fell into disarray after Operation Bluestar.[14]

Khalistan Commando Force

The Khalistan Commando Force (KCF) was founded in August 1986 under the leadership of Manbir Singh. The KCF principally targeted the Indian security forces such as the Border Security Force (BSF), the Central Reserve Police Force (CRPF), and other police forces. It targeted Hindus as well as Sikhs who opposed the Khalistan movement. The KCF funded itself through looting, bank robberies, and extortion. The group was responsible for some of the region's more notorious bank robberies, such as the 1987 robbery of the Punjab National Bank that netted Rs 5.7 crore (roughly $1.7 million in 1987 nominal dollars).[15] The KCF engaged in large-scale smuggling of weaponry from Pakistan. It was well organized, equipped, and trained and operated in coordination with other Sikh militant groups to enlarge the scope of their operations. The organization's ability to conduct operations was seriously degraded during Operation Black Thunder (to be described below).[16]

---

ensign/editorials/LTE/gingrich/gingrich014/dhaliwalVanSun.pdf, last accessed September 9, 2003.

[14] Pachnanda (2002), pp. 98–99. Also see *Jane's World Insurgency and Terrorism,* Vol. 17, "Sikh Separatists," March 7, 2003, available at www.janes.com.

[15] One crore equals 10 million Rupees. This calculation uses the approximate exchange rate of Rs 33 to 1 U.S. dollar for 1987.

[16] Pachnanda (2002), pp. 100–103. Also see *Jane's World Insurgency and Terrorism,* Vol. 17, "Sikh Separatists," March 7, 2003, available at www.janes.com.

Khalistan Liberation Force

Aroor Singh formed the Khalistan Liberation Force (KLF) in 1986. The KLF tended to use small arms (.303 and .315 rifles, 12 bore guns, revolvers, and pistols) in its operations, which it obtained principally through theft. It operated in the Punjab city of Amritsar as well as other localities. The KLF, like the other Khalistani militant organizations, financed itself through criminal activities. By 1990, the KLF's stature had been significantly degraded due to the loss of an important leadership figure.[17]

The KLF targeted Hindus, the Indian security forces (e.g., the BSF, CRPF, the police), and Sikhs who opposed the creation of Khalistan. It also targeted important persons from the commercial, industrial, and financial sectors, ostensibly to cripple efforts to economically vivify the state as well as to ensure its ability to extort money via its various racketeering efforts. The KLF generally attacked in strengths of 7–8 persons during the first half of the night and used trucks to escape. In addition to using guns to execute small groups of persons, it conducted random shooting sprees, deployed bombs in cinemas, and detonated car bombs.[18]

The KLF was responsible for a number of innovations. First, it adopted the practice of stealing vehicles in one place to commit crimes in a locality some 400–500 kilometers away. (A Deputy Inspector General of Police, Counter Intelligence Punjab, noted that because the police eventually made the connection between the theft of a car and an imminent militant attack, groups began purchasing vehicles to avoid alerting the authorities.[19]) It preferred using vehicles with more space for transporting weapons and explosives that could easily be concealed: The Ambassador car was a weapon of choice. The KLF took advantage of India's geography to operate and would coordinate its actions by phone in places as remote as Gujarat and Ma-

---

[17] Pachnanda (2002), pp. 103–119. Also see *Jane's World Insurgency and Terrorism,* Vol. 17, "Sikh Separatists," March 7, 2003, available at www.janes.com.

[18] Ibid.

[19] Interview with a former Deputy Inspector General of Police, Counter Intelligence Punjab, in June 2003.

harashtra.[20] Second, the KLF formed a suicide squad to assassinate high-value targets by using bombs attached to the cadres' bodies. Among their cadres was an expert in bomb construction. Third, as the KLF was a well-educated group, it developed a coded communications system for communications both within and outside the country.[21]

The KLF was also very agile and capable of operating throughout India. After 1992, it began financing itself through high-profile kidnappings in Mumbai, Tarpur, and Benares as well as bank robberies in Mumbai (Bombay), Allahabad, and Kolkata (formerly known as Calcutta). The KLF acquired a particular competence for kidnapping VIPs and raising large sums through ransoms. It kidnapped the chargé d'affaires of the Romanian Embassy. Cadres sometimes posed as truck drivers, which allowed them to move around the country unimpeded and without needing to seek shelter. Using fake passports, many cadres were able to enter foreign countries such as Pakistan, Nepal, Thailand, and the United Arab Emirates.[22] Reflecting the group's reach outside the country, diasporan Sikhs in Canada and the United Kingdom funded the KLF through the informal "hawala" channel to move funds.[23] The group also received financial assistance from Pakistan.[24]

---

[20] Pachnanda (2002), pp. 103–119. Also see *Jane's World Insurgency and Terrorism,* Vol. 17, "Sikh Separatists," March 7, 2003, available at www.janes.com.

[21] Ibid.

[22] Ibid.

[23] Hawala (also known as Hundi) is a remittance system that works outside of formal banking and financial channels. This system originated in South Asia and predates modern banking. It is now used throughout the world. Hawala uses the trust of its users coupled with extensive reliance upon family relationships, regional affiliations, and other such connections. The hawala system minimizes any reliance upon negotiable instruments and instead uses an elaborate communication system among the network members (hawaladars) to transfer money. For more details, see Interpol General Secretariat (2000).

[24] Pachnanda (2002), pp. 103–119. Also see *Jane's World Insurgency and Terrorism,* Vol. 17, "Sikh Separatists," March 7, 2003, available at www.janes.com.

The KLF was also a significant user of RDX.[25] Its actions comprised eight of the eleven cases where RDX was employed in Delhi and the Punjab. Its ability to use RDX with some level of expertise has been attributed to its ability to infiltrate the colleges, universities, and other educational institutes where the Sikh Student Federation had established strongholds.[26]

Campaigns of Violence

The above-noted Deputy Inspector General of Police (Counter Intelligence Punjab) explained that the Punjab militancy had four phases: (1) pre–Operation Bluestar, (2) post-Bluestar, (3) post–Black Thunder, and (4) post-1992 (when the insurgency was considered to be largely defeated). Each of these phases displayed different characteristics, resources, and tactics as well as alignments and motivations. During the first of these four phases, the militancy was localized and predominantly a rural phenomenon, apart from the city of Amritsar.

Amritsar was the first urban center where Sikh militancy flourished. It did so even in the early part of the militancy. This is in part because Jarnail Singh Bhindranwale moved his operations to Amritsar. Young recruits and cadres could easily execute attacks and take refuge in the Golden Temple. The narrow alleyways surrounding the temple complex afforded a number of operational opportunities for the cadres as well as easy escape routes. According to K.P.S. Gill, a senior officer in the Indian Police Service and former Director General of the Punjab Police, this was a typical modus operandi up until Operation Bluestar.[27]

---

[25] RDX is the acronym for Royal Demolition eXplosive. Its chemical name is 1,3,5-trinitro-1,3,5-triazine; however, it is also known as cyclonite or hexogen. It is a white powder and is very explosive.

[26] Pachnanda (2002), pp. 103–119. Also see *Jane's World Insurgency and Terrorism,* Vol. 17, "Sikh Separatists," March 7, 2003, available at www.janes.com.

[27] Conversations with K.P.S. Gill in August 2003.

Operation Bluestar changed everything, according to Gill. Amritsar remained a key center of terrorism, but the army and security forces maintained a consistent presence in the city and the temple that degraded the mobility of the cadres.[28] Operation Bluestar had other consequences of import. It precipitated widespread disaffection among Sikhs that Pakistan's Inter-Services Intelligence Directorate (ISI) sought to exploit. This dynamic of external support characterized the second phase of the militancy.[29] According to Indian analysts, the ISI encouraged the Khalistani groups to modernize their weapons and tactics and to urbanize the conflict. For example, Hardeep Singh Dhillon, the Senior Superintendent of Police Amritsar, explained in a 1992 interview with Joyce Pettigrew that the ISI provided Sikh insurgents with large supplies of AK-47s. (While initially the ISI was alleged to have sold the guns to the Sikh militants, it later gave them freely.)[30] From 1985 onward, according to a former Deputy Inspector General of Police, Counter Intelligence Punjab, the ISI mentored the groups and advised them to diversify the types of terrorism in which they engaged and to take the militancy into the urban areas.[31]

The ISI also helped to create a number of small, self-contained and well-equipped cells, according to Indian analysts.[32] By 1989, the militancy had spread into other important cities in India, such as

---

[28] Ibid.

[29] See Yaeger (1991), "Gleam of Light in Darkest Punjab" (1998), G. Singh (1996), and Burton and Fanney (2003).

[30] See interview with Dhillon, cited in Pettigrew (1995, pp. 105–106). Also see Smith (1996).

[31] As the above-given references suggest, the involvement of the ISI in nurturing these militants is well noted. This author's literature review did not find specific information buttressing the claims of a former Deputy Inspector General of Police, Counter Intelligence Punjab that the ISI explicitly encouraged militants to take their campaign to urban areas. In addition, previous work on Indian operations on urbanized terrain found no direct evidence to suggest that Pakistan had a deliberate policy of fomenting discord in India's cities. See Fair (2003).

[32] Written communication from a former Deputy Inspector General of Police, Counter Intelligence Punjab during our meeting in June 2003. See also Burton and Fanney (2003).

New Delhi, Kolkata, and Mumbai.[33] This urbanization effort was enabled by a key Sikh organization: the All India Sikh Students Federation (AISSF). The AISSF successfully infiltrated major educational institutions located in the Punjab's cities and towns. Colleges, universities, and other institutes became important locations for indoctrinating students as well as cultivating faculty who had particular areas of expertise. The success of this strategy is demonstrated by the fact that most of the prominent terrorist groups recruited more than 40 percent of their cadres from urban areas.[34]

There were also a number of factors that compelled the militancy to move into urban areas. First, the need to raise funds through extortion, kidnappings, and other criminal activities pushed the militant groups into towns and cities. The steady urbanization of the Punjab, which was generally concurrent with the period of militancy, facilitated this movement. As families (both Sikh and Hindu) that could afford to live in the cities chose to move, there were a number of opportunities to cultivate sympathetic families to provide shelter to the militants. This also meant that the targets were moving to the cities—that is, the Punjab's Hindus. Second, the militancy needed publicity and propaganda, and this was easily acquired through urban targeting. Third, the militants required facile interaction with and support from intellectuals and human rights activists, who were often based in cities. Fourth, the urban areas afforded militants the opportunity to network with organized criminal syndicates with operations in states other than the Punjab.[35] Finally, as odd as it may seem, the militants were attracted to the urban areas because they sought an urbane and posh lifestyle.[36]

---

[33] Interview with a former Deputy Inspector General of Police, Counter Intelligence Punjab, in June 2003.

[34] Written communication from a former Deputy Inspector General of Police, Counter Intelligence Punjab during our meeting in June 2003. See also the ethnography of Sikh militants by Puri, Judge, and Sekhon (1999).

[35] Written communication from a former Deputy Inspector General of Police, Counter Intelligence Punjab during our meeting in June 2003.

[36] Ibid.

New Delhi was choice terrain for the Khalistani militants because it is an independent federal entity situated at the intersection of the Indian states of Haryana, Uttar Pradesh, and Rajasthan. Militants could establish residences and hideouts in these states while conducting operations in New Delhi. This allowed the militants to exploit this legal "no man's land" and lack of coordination and cooperation among the various state law enforcement entities.[37]

After Operation Black Thunder, which will be described below, the police and other security forces began making significant headway in combating the militancy through a series of police innovations spearheaded by K.P.S. Gill. In the post-1992 phase, most analysts find that the insurgency had for the most part been eliminated. In this report, we will focus considerable attention on the post–Operation Bluestar phase and the institutional corrections pursued by K.P.S. Gill.

Militant Targeting and Innovations

In June 2003, the author met with numerous high-ranking police officers from Amritsar, Ludhiana, and elsewhere. These officers generally concurred that the most important terrorist targets were the political leadership. While several officers noted that industrialists were attractive targets also, they were seen as more easily replaceable than political leaders. The second most important target was the religious leadership. The third most significant set of targets comprised police officers, members of the judiciary, and others from the state apparatus. Random shootings were perhaps fourth in priority—but were the easiest to execute.

Militants did appear to evolve in their targeting and apparently had the opportunity to interact with other militant outfits, such as the LTTE when any of its members were in India. The police cited the fact that the militants began executing successive attacks as evidence of such interaction. For example, militants would plant an explosive in the casualty section of the hospital or in the cremation

---

[37] Interview with a former Deputy Inspector General of Police, Counter Intelligence Punjab in June 2003. Also see the ethnography of Sikh militants by Puri, Judge, and Sekhon (1999).

ground, set to detonate in the aftermath of a bombing elsewhere. This second attack anticipated the arrival of throngs of people as a result of the first attack. Sometimes this sequential bombing was strategic and aimed at high-level leadership: a bombing at a train station or other high-profile location would draw in police and civilian VIPs who would then be targeted by a second explosion.

Police officers interviewed for this report claimed that the Khalistanis learned a number of other things from the LTTE, such as the use of a series of antennas to amplify the detonation signal from a remote control. (The author could neither confirm nor disconfirm this through other sources.) With this method, they could detonate an explosive from 5 kilometers away in a rural area. According to these officers, the Babbar Khalsa also trained with the LTTE, from which they learned advanced remote detonation as well as the technique of planting a series of explosives during the construction of roads.[38] These officers further stated that the Sikh militants trained in the Merc School, owned by Frank Camper. Mr. Camper discusses his involvement with the Sikh militants in his autobiography (Camper, 1989).

Operations in Amritsar and Ludhiana

The militants had a number of important theaters, arguably the most important of which were Amritsar and Ludhiana. Amritsar was important because it is considered to be the spiritual center of the Sikhs. Any effort to secure an independent Sikh homeland that did not include Amritsar would be a failure ipso facto. Amritsar had symbolic importance to the global Sikh community. The attack on the Golden Temple during Operation Bluestar suggests some insights into the psychological significance of this city. Few Sikhs in the world would dispute that the deliberate use of the temple to house militants and serve as an impromptu armory and ammunitions dump was an inap-

---

[38] N.B.: Apart from interview data with Punjab police, the author could find no secondary source to buttress this claim that the LTTE interacted with the Khalistani militants.

propriate use of the site. However, the attack on what is perhaps the most sacred Sikh shrine was such an affront to Sikhs that it became an important source of political and militant mobilization for Sikhs throughout India and the world. Attacking the Golden Temple was tantamount to attacking Sikhism and the Sikh people—irrespective of the provocation.

Ludhiana was important because it was an up-and-coming industrial city in the Punjab. The Indian government encouraged investment and development in the Punjab to counter some of the claims from the 1970s that India sought to exploit the area for its agriculture while making no effort to cultivate other opportunities for it. Sikh militants were thought to target this important emerging industrial and commercial center to vitiate the central government's efforts to improve its image among the residents of the Punjab. Researchers at the Institute for Conflict Management in New Delhi suggest that targeting the business sector was an expedient means to deny the government any victory in its efforts to develop economic opportunities apart from the state's traditional agricultural sector.

According to police officials and analysts at the Institute for Conflict Management, Sikh militants in Ludhiana engaged primarily in extortion up through 1992. In 1992, an elected government came to power in the Punjab. Previously, it was governed from New Delhi because of the internal security situation. The manifestation of terrorism in Ludhiana transformed after the restoration of the state government. It began to include random civilian killings (e.g., with bombs), particularly of Hindus. Given Ludhiana's profile as an industrial center, workers were targeted. Many of these workers were migrants from other states and as such tended to be Hindus. Researchers at the Institute for Conflict Management suggested that the targeting of workers was intended to make it more difficult for companies to attract labor and to thereby degrade the viability of Ludhiana as an important industrial center. The militants also targeted multinational employees and their residential buildings for similar reasons.

Both the army and the police were involved at different times in providing security. The police tried to provide security through pickets. However, the militants easily targeted the police in these static positions. The army was also involved but was ineffectual in its efforts to establish a number of mobile columns moving around the city without adequate intelligence. The police, under the guidance of K.P.S. Gill, were eventually responsible for bringing order to Ludhiana. The Punjab police did not have the vehicles or manpower for motorized patrolling. However, they found that the foot mobile patrols were in any case superior to vehicle patrols. (They did not specify the reasons for this finding.)

Militancy in Amritsar and Operation Black Thunder

In 1986 and 1987, the government was keen to find a political solution to the crisis and commenced a sort of "peace process" with the

Figure 3.1
Map of Punjab (India)

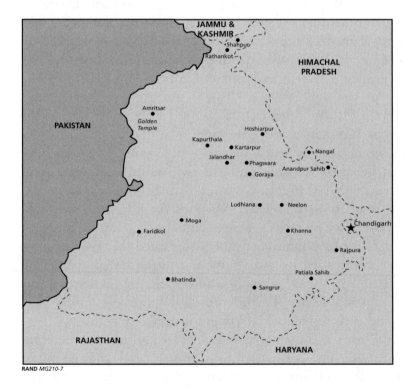

militants. In 1986, law and order in Punjab was the direct responsibility of the government in New Delhi. The central government pursued what Gill called "two-faced tactics," wherein it would attempt to strike deals with some militant factions while simultaneously putting pressure on them with enhanced police action. The government granted "selective immunity" to some militants, including associates of Bhindranwale who were taken into custody during Operation Bluestar. These varied tracks of dealing with militants created confusion for the police and the type of action that they should pursue.[39]

Gill writes that the Punjab police, despite this political disarray, committed themselves to what had become a drawn-out war with the militants. Between May 1987 and April 1988, the militants were killing, on average, 127 persons per month. The government continued to search for political solutions despite the intensity of the violence and the extent of the lawlessness. As a part of this strategy they released 40 high-profile prisoners in March 1988. These prisoners walked into the Golden Temple without hindrance, and one of them even became the head priest. The militants began fortifying the temple with internal defensive structures once again. The Golden Temple's management committee (the Shiromani Gurdwara Prabandhak Committee, or SGPC) was both passive and active in its support: some members were afraid of the terrorists and therefore did little to prevent their actions, while others directly assisted them.[40]

The government's strategy of negotiation with the militants did not mitigate the bloodshed. In March 1988, an unprecedented 288 people were slain, including 25 police personnel. This was followed by the killing of 259 persons in April, 25 of whom were policemen. The central government finally reversed its policy of political accom-

---

[39] See Gill (1999), pp. 14–16. While some of Gill's personal insights cannot be confirmed or disconfirmed in the secondary literature, there is a wide array of other accounts that are more general in nature. For more information about the impacts of Operation Bluestar, see Deora (1991, 1992) and Tully and Jacob (1991). For more general accounts of the insurgency and police actions there, see Kumar (2001), Ribeiro (1998), and Danewalia (1997).

[40] This information draws both from the author's June 2003 interview with Mr. Gill as well as Gill (1999). Other accounts of SGPC complicity include Brar (1993), Mahmood (1996), and Tully and Jacob (1991).

modation and again returned to a law enforcement approach.[41] The authorities once more concluded that some sort of action had to be taken to oust the militants from the temple. The government did not employ the army as it had done earlier; rather, it mobilized the police with backup from the National Security Guards (an anti-terrorist force) and other paramilitary forces.

It was hoped that this police action could be done without the inflammatory consequences of the 1984 army debacle, Operation Bluestar. Operation Black Thunder's objective was simple: clear the temple of militant forces. The operation succeeded on many fronts: it was economical, nearly bloodless in execution, and conducted with full media attention. The entire operation was completed within a week.[42] In contrast, Operation Bluestar was executed in a complete media blackout that fostered speculation and rumor throughout India and the world.

Gill explained the features of this successful operation. First, the police did a thoughtful appraisal of the temple and its environs and how operating in particular parts of the complex would resonate among the Sikh community. The Golden Temple compound could be divided into three rectangular areas: the serai (residential buildings for pilgrims and temple staff, a kind of rest house), the langar (a communal kitchen), and the temple (which included the inner sanctum, the Harminder Sahab). The police judged that they could enter the serai with very little protest. The langar is considered to be a very important institution in the Sikh religion, and action there was assessed to be more inflammatory than action within the rest house. Entering the temple, particularly the Harminder Sahab, would be the most provocative step. It is important to note that both the serai and the langar are outside the main temple structure. Taking into consideration these sensibilities, Gill proposed to take over the serai and the langar. The police would then conduct short and very limited attacks

---

[41] Gill (1999). See also Brar (1993), Mahmood (1996), and Tully and Jacob (1991).

[42] Gill, interview and (1999). See also Brar (1993), Mahmood (1996), and Tully and Jacob (1991).

within the temple and deny that such attacks occurred. These attacks would be done while in uniform and would aim to kill one or two militants per raid—*even though they would deny that such raids had occurred.* (While it is certainly curious that the forces would be uniformed while conducting attacks that would be denied, in the end, this contingency was not executed for reasons described below.)

The police first offered amnesty to any who surrendered. This was generally successful; however, a small number of militants escaped and took refuge in the temple's inner sanctum, the Harminder Sahab. The Harminder Sahab is located in the middle of the sacred pool with a walkway connecting the inner sanctum to the rest of the temple complex. Because this pathway can be easily defended, the militants in the inner sanctum had a robust position. Reportedly, no one shot at them as they made their way into the Harminder Sahab, perhaps in hopes of avoiding damage to the temple, as had occurred during Operation Bluestar.

The police conducted a prolonged siege against the temple to oust the militants. Gill recounts some of the methods used:

> We used various tactics to break their morale . . . Sometimes we enforced total silence followed by ammo and other loud noises. Chances for ceasefire were given during which one chap would go down to the pool to get water from the tank. We wanted to see if they had a container [for storing water]. We timed the water fetching during the ceasefire and assessed that there were some 8 or 9 militants in there as they were drinking from the bucket.

This allowed the police to ascertain the length of time the militants could stay there without food and water and calibrate the siege accordingly. This strategy culminated in a police victory.

As a police action, Operation Black Thunder was relatively minor and resulted in the capture of only a few militants. Shootouts in Amritsar still continued, and the type of violence committed actually escalated. After Black Thunder, the militants began planting explosives in scooters, bicycles, and other vehicles. These explosions were intended to kill randomly and to encourage people to leave the city. This situation persisted for three to four years.[43]

Viewed in the context of continued terrorist activity, it may be tempting to dismiss Operation Black Thunder as a failure of sorts; however, the operation structurally altered the militancy. Conducted in the watchful eyes of all media, Black Thunder revealed to the public aspects of the militancy that may not have been observed before with such clarity. Through the visibility of this operation, the Sikh people could see for themselves the depravity that went on within the walls of the Golden Temple. The Khalistan movement would never recover the veneer of religiosity that it had prior to the operation. Another important result of the operation was that the Golden Temple and gurdwaras (Sikh religious temples) were thereafter denied to the militants as a source of sanctuary and operational basing.[44]

Innovations of the Punjab Police

Gill offered a number of criticisms of the state's efforts to combat Sikh violence during the early days of the militancy. The various security forces operated independently of each other and in ways that were highly compartmentalized. This operational disconnect affected the ability of the forces to perform efficiently, and it shaped the public perception of these forces. Citing Amritsar as an example, Gill explained that the local community saw the Punjab police as a "Sikh force" largely because police draw from a local, predominantly Sikh, labor force. When the federal entity, the Central Reserve Police Force, was deployed to the Amritsar area, the officers were seen as being there to protect the Hindus. That the forces did not operate together fostered the public perception that they had particular constituencies. Gill laments that at one point the failure of these forces to communicate nearly resulted in one firing upon the other.

---

[43] Gill interview, June 2003.

[44] Gill, interview and (1999). See also Brar (1993), Mahmood (1996), and Tully and Jacob (1991), as well as Fair (2003).

Gill also noted that while there was extensive police deployment throughout the Punjab, these deployments were static, presenting easy targets and opportunities to kill police. When Gill took over the force (then numbering 35,000), between 40 and 50 percent of it was dedicated to static duties such as police pickets and checkpoints:

> These barricades . . . at best . . . helped create the illusion of security among the general public through massive and visible police presence; at worst, they provided terrorists with easy targets for drive-by shootings, or for a "weapon-snatching" raid. . . . Convinc[ing] officers of the Punjab Police that this was a waste of human resources was difficult. Even those who were convinced said that it was impossible to dismantle and disband the pickets, since the political leadership thought this to be the best strategy for policing.[45]

In summation, Gill argued that such picketing depleted manpower, rendered them vulnerable to militant attacks, was costly to maintain, and irrelevant when measured in the results it produced. Easy killing of the police forces furthered the perception that the government was ineffectual and unable to protect the populace.

Terrorist activities, coupled with the inability of the security forces to restore civil order, shook the confidence of Punjab's residents that the government could contain the militant threat. This resulted in public unwillingness to provide intelligence out of fear of reprisals by the militants, who had demonstrated competence in liquidating not only suspected informants but also their entire families. Without critical intelligence, the security forces were increasingly ineffectual, which furthered the decline in public confidence.

It was into this environment that K.P.S. Gill entered the conflict and began his own initiatives to address the varied shortcomings. It should be noted that while Mr. Gill has gathered much fame for quelling the militancy, he has numerous detractors. A number of human rights organizations charged him with being personally responsible for the widespread occurrences of rape, torture, and "en-

---

[45] Gill (1999), p. 20.

counter killings." Critics further point out that he remained at his post of Director General of Police in Punjab for two years despite these allegations.[46] While the author is aware of the controversy surrounding Mr. Gill, his approach to the Punjab militancy offers a number of insights that will be of interest to readers of this report.

K.P.S. Gill took over the position of Director General of Police in Punjab only a few weeks prior to launching Operation Black Thunder. After that victory, Gill proceeded to make a number of other key changes in the Punjab police force to enhance its counterterrorism capabilities. The first battle that Gill fought was against the state and central authorities to ensure that the police were adequately armed to confront the militants. While the militants had AK series weapons, the police had only .303 rifles. Gill encountered considerable political resistance to the notion, but some progress was made in improving the arming of the force. Second, Gill encouraged an expansion of the force by an additional 25,000 personnel. This brought the end-strength to 60,000. Third, Gill pushed through changes in the ratio of mobile to static and nonproductive manpower assignments.[47]

Third, Gill redeployed manpower to mobile units that patrolled areas with a known militant presence. This satisfied the public need for visibility of security forces and also degraded terrorist mobility. Another innovation was "focal point patrolling." This was in many ways a force multiplier whereby all available manpower and vehicles would be amassed at a particular place at a particular time. This gave the illusion of a saturation of forces that in fact did not exist.[48] Gill explained during our interview another variant of this tactic, in which police meetings would be called in the middle of the night at a sensitive location. All police officers of the district, senior and subordinate, would be required to attend. This would result in a clustering of personnel and vehicles at one locality. The police called this "Operation

---

[46] Mahmood (1996), p. 208

[47] Gill (1999), p. 20.

[48] Ibid., p. 21.

Night Dominance," and, as Gill explained, it was an important effort to bolster public confidence that the terrorists did not own the night.[49]

Fourth, Gill had to deal with the massive infiltration of the police forces by Sikh militants that had occurred over the course of the militancy as well as the perception that some of the police had been compromised. On the one hand, there were certainly some individuals who had been recruited by the militants. The other issue of perception was more subtle and difficult to deal with. Because the central police forces tended to be called in from the outside, they had a relatively small percentage of Sikhs in their ranks. They often displayed an anti-Sikh bias or were perceived to do so. As explained above, this resulted in part because the state and central police forces did not interact. Although identifying some of the features of the problems was simple, executing a solution was more difficult.[50]

It was important to keep potentially compromised personnel out of counterterrorism duties, but it was also important to do so discreetly to avoid further aggravation of public and police sentiment. The challenge was to continually identify compromised personnel and redeploy them to tasks that did not jeopardize counterterrorism activities. The police leadership also made efforts to ensure that officers leading operations were both free of bias (and perceived to be free of bias) and well versed in the dangers that fundamentalist thinking posed to the integrity of the state.[51] Gill did not elaborate on exactly how this was done or how the effectiveness was measured.

Gill also addressed the ways in which the various security forces operated independently. The Punjab police were resentful of some of the central forces because the local police had been depicted as the enablers of the terrorist movement and this disinclined them from working with the central forces. There were also the typical "turf" wars that large institutions tend to wage because of the implications

---

[49] Ibid.

[50] Ibid., pp. 22–23.

[51] Ibid.

that their operations have on budgetary outlays and political outcomes. One of the most severe problems in this system was the fate of intelligence. Information was not shared with the other forces even if it had clear operational implications for other forces. To address this lack of multidirectional intelligence flow, Gill implemented a structure to foster systematic intelligence collection and analysis.[52]

Gill, speaking to the author in September 2002, elaborated upon these intelligence operations. To coordinate the activities of the intelligence agencies involved in the Punjab militancy, the principals convened regular meetings. These agencies included: the Intelligence Bureau; the Research and Analysis Wing; the various state intelligence agencies; the Central Bureau of Investigation (which investigates serious crimes); representatives from New Delhi as well as from all of the Indian states that were affected; the Directors of Revenue and Narcotics as well as Customs and Excise; and any other entity that was conceivably involved with containing the movement.[53] Other initiatives pursued by Gill were the formation and utilization of joint interrogation teams to ensure that information would flow to all agencies involved. In Amritsar he institutionalized a process through which the local police and the central police force worked together. This proved very effective and was instituted across the Punjab.[54]

As the general environment improved and fostered a renewed confidence among the populace that the security forces were in control, the police were better positioned to develop on-the-ground intelligence assets. Public confidence and support enabled the police to capture militants who they could turn into informants. The police were also able to recruit citizens who could identify the militants. These individuals were known as "spotters" and were critical in identifying the terrorists to the police. Gill noted that getting these spotters was a difficult task despite the improved situation. They tended to be either former associates of the militants or people who had

---

[52] Ibid., pp. 23–24.

[53] Gill interview, September 2002.

[54] Gill (1999), pp. 23–24.

come from the same village as the militants. Another class of spotters comprised persons who either survived attacks or were victims' relatives and were in a position to identify the assailants.[55]

As a result of changes that were implemented after Operation Black Thunder, the Punjab police were able to carry out operations that were specific to a given area, a particular gang, or a terrorist activity. Progressively, the terrorists lost the initiative, and over time the security forces increasingly regained control. While the militants are still capable of organizing random attacks on soft targets, they can no longer do so with impunity. Even if they succeeded in executing a major operation, the security forces could mount an effective counterterrorist operation in which the responsible group would be targeted, as would its safe houses anywhere in India. The capacity of individual terrorists and prominent groups to act had been severely degraded.

The above-mentioned Deputy Inspector General of Police, Counter Intelligence Punjab noted several other innovations introduced in the Punjab police during the Sikh militancy. He explained that bomb threats had increasingly become a problem in the Punjab. The terrorists would detonate motorcycle- and bicycle-borne bombs in bazaars and market areas. The police enhanced the monitoring of areas where such vehicles were parked. Police also began patrolling high-value target areas (e.g., railway and bus stations) both in uniform and out. They also tried to harden targets by using drop gates and barriers. At important buildings (e.g., television stations, radio broadcasting facilities, government buildings) and VIP residences with multiple access ways, they would block all but one and narrow the point of entry.

As Gill's account of "Operation Night Dominance" and "focal point patrolling" suggests, the police used deception as a force multiplier. A former Deputy Inspector General of Police, Counter Intelligence Punjab offers another example. In their efforts to assemble anti-sabotage teams, the police needed "sniffer dogs" that could detect ex-

---

[55] Gill interview, June 2003.

plosive materials. However, sniffer dogs were expensive and required long lead times to train. The Punjab police found that they could use regular dogs as a part of their deception campaign to give the impression that they had many more sniffer dogs than they actually had. The public could not distinguish the difference between the ordinary and trained bomb-detecting canines.

The police also conducted combing operations in daylight, making use of specific intelligence rather than the general search procedures that typified the previous manner of policing. These operations would typically be done on a Sunday, when all residents were likely to be at home, and were understood to be both preventive as well as detective in nature. This tactic was preventive in the sense that it would discourage militants from taking refuge in particular homes and would discourage families from willingly providing such assistance. It was detective in that it afforded the police the opportunity to detain for questioning militants who were identified in this process. Another attempt at monitoring residential areas included regimes requiring the verification of tenants. (New Delhi still does this.) Under this policy, landlords were required to confirm the identity of their tenants and to register this information with the appropriate police authorities.

As indicated throughout this chapter, Sikh religious institutions such as the gurdwaras and their associated rest houses, or serais, had become a common place for militants to take refuge. Operations against entrenched militants posed enormous public relations problems and could further inflame the sensibilities of the Sikh community. To avoid further hostility among the Sikhs and the possibility of radicalizing them into the militancy, the police had to tread carefully on this issue. To this end, the above-referenced former Deputy Inspector General of Police, Counter Intelligence Punjab explained that the police executed random searches of gurdwara complexes, including the serais. These operations were done both to deter militants from using religious institutions for sanctuary and to identify and capture militants who present before they became so entrenched in the structure that more aggressive action would be required to dislodge them.

Summary

The Sikh experiences in the Punjab offer a number of insights. First, comparing Operation Bluestar and Operation Black Thunder reveals very different approaches to understanding the impact of such operations on the global Sikh community. Operation Bluestar paid little heed to the fact that authorities could operate in parts of the complex with relatively little outrage, while entering the temple would be very provocative. Second, Operation Bluestar was conducted in a media blackout. This did not afford the army and the security forces any opportunity to manage the way in which the Indian and global publics understood the execution of the operation until well after it was completed. Operation Black Thunder, conducted in the full view of the world through maximal media coverage, gave the security forces ample occasion to demonstrate to the world the militants' utilization of the Golden Temple as a criminal sanctuary. It also made the conduct of the security forces visible to all, which likely discouraged questionable behavior on the part of the security forces and possibly on the part of the militants, the vast majority of whom evacuated the temple without incident.

The Punjab case is illustrative for other reasons as well. The Punjab police, under the guidance of K.P.S. Gill, demonstrate the utility of deception as a force multiplier in a resource- and manpower-constrained environment. The Punjab experiences also raise important questions about the value of pickets and other static uses of police personnel versus mobile patrols. While prima facie one may imagine that a heavy presence of police forces throughout a city may encourage public confidence, this was not the case in Punjab. The police were very vulnerable in these static positions. The ease with which they were targeted apparently degraded the public's perception that the security forces were in control. The Punjab police also found that when adopting mobile patrol options, foot patrols were more effective than vehicle patrols.

The Punjab case, like the Sri Lanka case, demonstrates the importance of educational institutions in the recruitment of militants, the recruitment of faculty with specific skills and expertise, and the dissemination of a political narrative that supports the aims of the militants. Because universities tend to be located in cities and towns, they offer an important node in bringing campaigns to the city. The universities also offer the opportunity for militant organizations and their sympathizers to network with intellectuals who in turn produce scholarship that reflects the worldview and equities of the militants.

The diaspora emerges as an important strategic ally in the Khalistan case as well. The diaspora functions to generate political support within the governments of the various host countries. Its members remit money and other resources to institutions at home to fuel the conflict. They also provide key logistical support to facilitate the involvement of external state support.

This study reveals the importance of groups operating as allies of militancy within the United States and other western states. It also raises important questions for policing in urban areas. Some of this may be valuable as the United States engages in global policing operations. For example, should U.S. forces be used in static police operations or mobile patrols? As the United States tries to assemble indigenous police forces, how does one avoid the perception that those forces are protecting the equities of a particular group? What are the tradeoffs in using local police forces versus a centralized police force? These concerns will be elaborated at length in the concluding chapter of this report.

The Indian experience also identifies several problems that may exist within the domestic security apparatus of the United States. It also offers insight into the types of apparatus that the United States and its partners may seek to establish in Iraq and Afghanistan. As the Punjab case demonstrates, terrorists can easily operate across different states to exploit any lapse in operational and intelligence coordination among the agencies. It also shows how important it is that central government forces interact in an integrated manner with local forces to avoid the belief that the "outside" forces protect the interests of one party and the local forces protect other parties in minority-dominated areas. Integrated operations also need to ensure that intelligence and other information is shared in a rational manner and that tasks are assigned to the most appropriate force—not just the force that came across the lead.

CHAPTER FOUR

Pakistan

Preview of the Argument

This chapter examines two campaigns of urban violence in Pakistan: the anti-state violence of the Muttehida (formerly Muhajir) Qaumi Movement (MQM), and the sectarian violence perpetrated mostly by militant Sunni outfits against Pakistan's minority Shi'a population. Examination of these case studies generally found that innovation among these militant groups was relatively flat. In many ways, the process of urbanization itself and the various social and economic changes that accompanied this wide-scale movement to Pakistan's cities precipitated these forms of violence. Because those forms were generally urban in conception, the various movements learned to exploit the terrain of the city. For example, the MQM gains great utility in disrupting the conduct of business in Karachi, Pakistan's commercial and economic hub. Sectarian militant outfits take advantage of public religious processions (e.g., Shi'a Muharram rituals) through urban passageways to target Shi'a and cause violent riots. As these movements were generally coincident with the spread of small arms in Pakistan, these outfits have had little problem acquiring light machine guns and rocket launchers. However, assassination and terrorizing the residents remain the weapons of choice for these organizations.

Despite the relative lack of sophistication of these groups, the Pakistani security forces have not evolved effective tools to counter them. This is in part because of the poorly trained and inadequately equipped police force and in part because the local police are not well informed by the more competent and highly resourced central intelligence agencies. In addition, because the police tend to be corrupt, citizens will generally avoid any encounter with them, as it is certain to be unpleasant and/or an extortion opportunity. As a consequence, there is an adversarial relationship between the population being policed and the police force. Data obtained from a community-policing effort in Punjab suggested that such an approach has a number of palliative impacts—mostly through bettering relations between the police and the citizens and through creating a greater civic awareness among the populace. What is clear from these two cases is that Pakistan requires much assistance in fortifying its internal security apparatus. As Pakistan is a key state in the global war on terrorism, robust law enforcement and investigative capabilities will be required to enable Pakistan to meet the most expansive expectations held by Washington and others.

Introduction to the Cases

Pakistan's persistent prosecution of a proxy war in Indian-held Kashmir is well known. What is less appreciated is that Pakistan is itself a victim of violence and has been for decades. In fact, President Pervez Musharraf has repeatedly claimed that internal threats to Pakistan are perhaps the most serious peril it faces.[1] Pakistan's internal security has been greatly affected by external events (such as the Iranian Revolution, the Iran-Iraq War, and the Soviet invasion of Afghanistan) as well as by its own internal political and military dynamics. The sectarian conflict between the Shi'a and Sunni Muslim sects and the inter-ethnic violence perpetrated by and against Pakistan's Muhajir community have been manifestations of violence that has nearly crippled Pakistan. The latter type of violence has been most concentrated in Karachi and other urban areas of the Pakistani

---

[1] See "Fighting Terrorism," *The Dawn,* March 7, 2004.

province of Sindh. Both of these particular kinds of violence are nearly exclusively urban in nature.

This chapter will first detail both the phenomenon of sectarian and inter-ethnic violence as well as the groups behind these menaces. Next it details those elements of Pakistan's force structure that have been used in internal security operations. In the third section, the chapter analyzes two very different sets of experiences with these forms of violence.

The chapter explores Pakistan's experiences through two different cases. The first case is comprised of the ongoing violence in Karachi that has turned that important port city into an urban battlefield since the early 1980s. We will look particularly at a period of time when the Pakistani army and the security forces were deployed to Karachi to restore law and order. This experience is illuminating not for its success but rather for its abysmal failure. There are many facets of that operation, which at first blush appear to resonate with current police efforts in Iraq by U.S. and other forces.

The second case will be comprised of experiences in experimental community policing that the District Inspector General, Azhar Hassan Nadeem, conducted in the early 1990s in the district of Gujranwala (Punjab). Nadeem adapted a British community-policing model that he came across while doing his graduate work in criminology in the United Kingdom. Nadeem adopted this system to accommodate the Islamic and other social and cultural facets that are specific to Pakistan and implemented the program during his tenure in Gujranwala.

What is notable about Nadeem's experience is that he built into this test case methods of evaluating the process. In advance of implementing a community-policing model in a particular test locality, the police fielded a survey to ascertain the attitudes of the residents towards the police, their own relationship and responsibility in securing their safety, their safety-related practices, and their perceptions of their environment and crime. They fielded the same set of survey questions some six months after the program had been functioning to find out how public perceptions had been affected by the model. The survey, with a sample size of 200, may not have been executed with technical perfection.[2] It is nonetheless illuminating, particularly since many of the police/community structures Nadeem identifies could conceivably be adapted to environments with social and cultural complexity similar to that of Pakistan (e.g., Iraq).

The Twin Urban Menaces of Sectarian and Inter-Ethnic Violence

Sectarian violence within Pakistan had its nascence in the overlapping developments in the region: the Iranian Revolution, the Iran-Iraq War, and the Soviet invasion of Afghanistan, coupled with the consequences of urbanization and other demographic pressures. The Iranian Revolution animated the political aspirations of Shi'a communities in Pakistan and elsewhere. Tehran, in an effort to spread its revolution, financed key Shi'a political organizations in Pakistan. The Iran-Iraq War of 1980 made Pakistan a proxy theater wherein both Iran and Iraq fought for dominance through the financing of Shi'a and Sunni sectarian organizations. States such as Saudi Arabia and the United Arab Emirates also stepped into the fray, funding Sunni organizations to temper Iran's influence. The activities of Saudi Arabia and other Arab states became more intense with the Soviet invasion of Afghanistan, bolstered by active support for this involvement from the United States.[3]

The 1979 Soviet invasion of Afghanistan was a watershed event for Pakistan and key institutions such as the army and its important external intelligence agency, the Inter-Services Intelligence Directorate (ISI). Analysts usually focus on the significance of this event in terms of its transformation of the struggle in Indian-held Kashmir. However, one of the less-appreciated consequences of the events in Afghanistan was the vast infrastructure established by the United States, the ISI, Saudi Arabia, and others to combat the Soviets in this theater. This infrastructure not only transformed the dispute in

---

[2] There is too little information about the methodology to ascertain the technical quality of the effort.

[3] See, for example, International Crisis Group (2002).

Kashmir but also permanently changed the relations among Pakistan's various sectarian groups.

One of the key institutions in this multifront "jihad" against the Soviet Union was the once prestigious institution of Islamic learning, the madrassah system. Traditionally, the madrassah was a religious institution focusing on seminary studies. A madrassah provides free Islamic education in accordance with the teachings of its particular sect. (Madrassahs are typically connected to mosques with specific sectarian leanings.) Poorer students will typically live at the madrassahs and receive boarding and lodging for free. While middle-class and wealthy families may also send their children (typically sons) to madrassahs for Quran lessons, these children are usually day students. The traditional madrassah curriculum includes learning how to read, memorize, and recite the Quran properly. Students will also study exegeses and other aspects of Islamic studies at more advanced levels. Graduates of this system have few labor market opportunities outside of mosques and other madrassahs.[4] Traditionally, madrassahs were not associated with indoctrination for militant activities.

As a result of both the U.S.-driven efforts to turn the schools into a jihadi production base to roll back the Soviet invasion of Afghanistan and General Zia's utilization of this process to consolidate his own power base, the madrassah system was dramatically transformed in Pakistan. The age-old system was further distorted when Shi'a and Sunni communities competed against one another for support, patronage, and visibility from the Pakistani regime as well as from sources of external support. Consequently, the sectarian divisions along which madrassahs were organized became militarized, and this trajectory of militarization was amply aided by Iran and the Gulf states, which financed the sectarian madrassahs of their choice.[5]

Sectarian violence in Pakistan between Shi'a and Sunni Muslims is urban in origin and manifestation. Specific localities within the Punjab typified this new phenomenon as it underwent extensive ur-

---

[4] Ibid.

[5] Ibid.

banization in the 1970s and 1980s.[6] The movement toward cities resulted from population pressure upon the land from the large number of families that could not sustain themselves via their agricultural activities. Urbanization was also propelled by the Gulf oil boom. The rise of expatriate labor and corresponding remittances enabled families to migrate to the Punjab's urban centers, and the new conurbations developed on the edge of agricultural lands.[7]

This pattern of migration fundamentally altered traditional patterns of authority and in turn restructured sectarian relations. The newcomers to the urban areas tended to be Sunni Muslims, and they formed a nascent urban Sunni middle class. As these new migrants were only marginally tied to the surrounding agricultural economy, they were not directly part of the regional rural feudal power structure. (In Pakistan, the rural feudal power structure is an important driver of electoral politics and its influence extends even into the urban area. Newcomers seeking to establish political influence must deal with the landed elite that governs the political system in question.) This burgeoning Sunni middle class sought influence in the local politics consonant with its demographic and economic strength. This required challenging the political control of members of the landed elite, who were Shi'a landlords in many areas of the Punjab (e.g., Jhang, Kabirwala).[8]

Sunni political entrepreneurs used sectarian sentiment to militarize the Sunni identity of the middle class and to accentuate the Shi'a identity of the landed elite. In urban areas like Jhang, Shi'a landlords and members of the Sunni middle class have been competing for the allegiance of Sunni peasants since the mid-1980s. In these same areas, numerous militant seminaries have been established which have transformed these localities into sectarian battlefields.[9]

---

[6] Zaman (1998).

[7] Nasr (January 2000), Zaman (1998).

[8] Ibid.

[9] Ibid.

Sectarian violence in Pakistan has become a significant law and order problem that has attracted the highest level of involvement from the Pakistani authorities. However, as there is often overlapping membership between the anti-Shi'a groups with a sectarian focus and groups acting in Afghanistan or in Kashmir, cracking down on these anti-Shi'a sectarian-oriented groups is sometimes quite difficult. Key anti-Shi'a groups include the Lashkar-e-Jhangvi (LeJ) and the Sipah-e-Sahaba-e-Pakistan (SSP).[10] The primary Shi'a sectarian groups are the Tehrik-e-Jaffria Pakistan (TJP) and Sipah-e-Muhammad Pakistan (SMP). Unlike the LeJ and SSP, which share membership with traditional "jihadi" groups, there are no Shi'a organizations fighting in the Kashmir or Afghanistan theaters. Below we provide an overview of the key groups involved.

Major Sectarian Militant Organizations

Sipah-e-Sahaba-e-Pakistan and the Lashkar-e-Jhangvi. Sipah-e-Sahaba-e-Pakistan (SSP) dates back to the early 1980s and follows hard-line Deobandi and Wahhabi traditions and philosophy. This organization was specifically formed in the early to middle 1980s (the exact date is uncertain) in response to the Iranian revolution. The Iranian Revolution emboldened Pakistan's Shi'a community, which is estimated to comprise anywhere from 15 to 25 percent of the population.[11] To counter the rising influence of Tehran and the bolstered political initiative of Pakistan's Shi'a, Saudi Arabia and other Gulf states contributed heavily to Sunni mosques and religious institutions. These Arab states contributed through direct government channels as well as through charitable foundations. A consequence of this involvement was that particular strands of Sunni Islam were promoted, particularly Wahhabism and Deobandism, at the expense

---

[10] The SSP, upon being banned in January 2003, reportedly reformed under a new name: Millat-e-Islamia Pakistan.

[11] Pakistan does not conduct its census in the heavily Shi'a populated Northern Areas, which means that an exact enumeration of the Shi'a population is not possible.

of the more traditional strands of Barelvi Islam with its Sufi tradition and background.[12]

As noted above, settlement and urbanization patterns had already fuelled resentment among the Shi'a feudal elite and encouraged power-hungry Sunnis to mobilize sectarian identity to diminish the stature of these Shi'a landholding families. This tendency was encouraged by individuals such as Zia ul Haq, who welcomed militarized Sunni activities to counter those of his arch-nemesis Benazir Bhutto, whose family had ties to the Shi'a landed elite in Sindh.[13]

Anti-Shi'a unrest among the Sunnis was activated and channeled through the formation of the SSP around 1985. In the context of the Iranian Revolution and the rise of anti-Shi'a sentiment, the Shi'a organized the political organization Tehrik-e-Nifaz-e-Fiqah-e-Jaffria (TNFJ). The TNFJ, as will be described below, was not a militant organization but gave rise to a number of militant outfits such as the Tehrik-e-Jaffria Pakistan (TJP) and the Sipah-e-Muhammed Pakistan (SMP). Fighting between these rival sectarian factions set off a bloody cycle of revenge killing that has continued to challenge Pakistan's social fabric ever since. The particular objectives of the SSP involve establishing Pakistan as a Sunni state in which Shi'a are officially declared "Kafir" (nonbelievers). They have attacked Iranian targets in Pakistan because Iran is believed to be the source of support for Pakistan's Shi'a.[14]

The SSP's former leader, Maulana Azam Tariq, was detained in October 2001 following large and violent pro-Taliban protests. The SSP, despite being a terrorist group, has episodically fielded candidates in elections. Most recently this occurred in October 2002, when Tariq successfully contested and won a seat for the National Assembly (MNA) and made the SSP a coalition partner in the federal government. Tariq, denying charges that he was a terrorist, declared that

---

[12] See *Jane's World Insurgency and Terrorism,* Vol. 16, "Sipha-e-Sahaba," November 21, 2002, available at www.janes.com. See also "Lashkar-e-Jangvi," in the same volume. See also Jalalzai (1998).

[13] Ibid.

[14] Ibid.

his organization has forsworn violence. However, during the author's fieldwork in Pakistan (August 2003), no interviewee entertained these assertions as credible. Moreover, it was widely believed that this otherwise notorious criminal was allowed to contest elections because he was willing to support the regime's preference for prime minister.[15] In October 2003, Tariq was assassinated.[16]

The SSP has established commands in Pakistan's main cities, reflecting its primarily urban base. Its stronghold has traditionally been the Punjab and has some 500 offices in that province alone. It has increasingly established itself in the Northwest Frontier Province, mostly through the SSP-affiliated madrassahs, which comprise the majority of foreign-funded Sunni schools in Pakistan. The organization draws its funding from Sunni businessmen in the Punjab—often in the form of protection money—and from wealthy individuals in Pakistan. It is also believed that the SSP obtains funding from Saudi Arabia.[17]

The SSP is believed to have had several members who trained with and assisted the Taliban in Afghanistan. The SSP also has some sort of connection with the Kashmir-oriented militant group called the Jaish-e-Mohammed (JM). SSP's chairman declared that the SSP is "hand in hand . . . shoulder to shoulder with JM in jihad." The SSP also articulated its support for other Kashmir-oriented groups, including the Taliban and even al Qaeda. Interlocutors in Pakistan view this stated allegiance with Kashmir-oriented groups (e.g., LeT and JM) with considerable cynicism because they have observed that Pakistani criminal and sectarian groups cloak themselves in the rhetoric of Kashmir to gain insulation from action by the security appara-

---

[15] Interviews with Pakistani analysts, journalists, and retired military personnel in July and August 2003.

[16] See Asghar and Syed (2003).

[17] See *Jane's World Insurgency and Terrorism,* Vol. 16, "Sipha-e-Sahaba," November 21, 2002, available at www.janes.com. See also "Lashkar-e-Jangvi," in the same volume. See also Jalalzai (1998).

tus. Such interlocutors believe groups claiming affiliation with the jihad in Kashmir are immune to government sanction.[18]

The SSP is also linked with the LeJ, and in fact it is difficult to distinguish operationally between the two. The LeJ was formed in 1996 as a "death squad" for the SSP, and it consequently shares the that group's political objectives. The LeJ has its own command structure but shares the SSP's urban support base. The LeJ is primarily an urban guerilla group with small cells (with eight or fewer members) operating independently of each other. While the LeJ is believed to have only 300 or so cadres, its support base is rooted to the 3,000–6,000 members of the SSP. The LeJ primarily funds itself through criminal activity such as protection rackets or robbing Shi'a banks and other business establishments. It, like its parent the SSP, has benefited from the funding that Saudi and other wealthy Arabs channeled through Karachi.[19]

The SSP and the LeJ also have similar modes of operation. The SSP has two general modes of attack: assassination of prominent Shi'a or SSP opponents and massacres. Massacres are typically executed with an SSP cadre opening fire on large gatherings of Shi'a at mosques, at wedding parades, or during important Shi'a religious celebrations such as Muharram, when Shi'a participate in a number of daylong processions. The LeJ also conducts massacres and executions and has particularly targeted Shi'a professionals (e.g., doctors, lawyers, teachers, party leadership, lobbyists, and scholars). The LeJ has been blamed for attacking several Western targets and has been implicated in the kidnapping and murder of *Wall Street Journal* reporter Daniel Pearl.[20] However, interlocutors in Pakistan were dubious that the LeJ was involved in such targeting. These informants believed that the government was blaming these attacks on the LeJ to

---

[18] Ibid.

[19] Ibid.

[20] Ibid.

give itself cover to liquidate the group, which has long vexed Pakistan's police and other security apparatus.[21]

The LeJ and SSP have access to a full range of armaments. Both have access to the AK series of rifles. The LeJ also has rockets, landmines, explosives, and other forms of weaponry available from Afghanistan and China. LeJ cadres are drawn from SSP-run madrassahs, and many served in Afghanistan prior to October 2001. During Operation Enduring Freedom, the LeJ lost its most important training base in Afghanistan at Sarobi. It still has important training bases in Muridke and in Kabirwala in Pakistan. However, these have come under close scrutiny and have probably undergone significant downsizing. SSP cadres also served in Afghanistan with the Taliban, mostly as foot soldiers, and received training in mountain guerilla warfare. Some were selected to train with al Qaeda, where they received advanced bomb making instruction.[22]

Shi'a Sectarian Groups: Sipah-e-Muhammed-Pakistan and Tehrik-e-Jaffria Pakistan. As noted above, Tehran encouraged the Shi'a of Pakistan to politicize their identity as a part of Tehran's larger effort to export its Shi'a Islamic revolution and encourage Shi'a to mobilize against Sunnis wherever possible. By the time that the resistance to the Soviet occupation of Afghanistan was under way, a Shi'a political organization came into being with the encouragement of Iran. Its name, Tehrik Nifaz Fiqah-e-Jaffria (TNFJ), was derived from a Shi'a school of jurisprudence and rankled the sensibilities of Sunni clerics and militants. This organization gave rise to Shi'a militant organizations, the Tehrik-e-Jaffria Pakistan (TJP) and the Sipah-e-Mohammed-Pakistan (SMP).

The violence between Sunni and Shi'a escalated throughout the 1980s and became particularly virulent toward the end of that decade as Punjabi militants began returning from combat in Afghanistan.

---

[21] Interviews with Pakistani analysts, journalists, and retired military personnel in July and August 2003.

[22] See *Jane's World Insurgency and Terrorism,* Vol. 16, "Sipha-e-Sahaba," November 21, 2002, available at www.janes.com. See also "Lashkar-e-Jangvi," in the same volume. See also Jalalzai (1998).

Such individuals were well armed and trained in guerilla warfare. More important, they were steeped in radical Sunni doctrine and were acclimated to the high levels of violence in Afghanistan, where they frequently slaughtered Shi'a with the Taliban's encouragement. It was within this context that the Shi'a community underwent considerable debate about the role and sanction of violence. Militants within the TJP wanted the organization to sanction anti-Sunni actions. The organization had already developed a number of internal fissures. One faction followed the teachings of Ayatollah Madari and retained the name of TNFJ. The other faction kept the name TJP and sought to maintain a status as essentially a religious organization without political or military moorings.[23]

A militarized Shi'a organization led by Maulana Abbas, the SMP, emerged in 1993. Abbas became convinced that the Shi'a clergy would not endorse a policy of violence against the Sunnis. While the SMP and TJP had similar membership, it was the SMP that quickly became known as the militant Shi'a branch. However, the SMP became mired in internal squabbles over leadership, political orientation, and the role of violence. In 1996 a member ordered the assassination of a senior leader because of his conciliatory posture toward other groups within Pakistan. During most of that year, the SMP engaged in a cycle of internal revenge killings.[24]

The SMP currently claims some 3,000 armed members, many of whom are also TJP members. SMP principally aims to establish a Shi'a government in Pakistan where Shi'a may be protected from Sunni excesses and theological rulings. While it does espouse wider goals such as the liberation of Jerusalem, its activities have been limited to Pakistan. Its leader, Ghulam Naqvi, was sought in connection with 30 murders and other violent incidents. He was subsequently arrested in 1996 but remains the group's leader from prison. The SMP's operational command was retarded by his arrest. The group is

---

[23] Ibid.

[24] Ibid.

no longer thought to be an organized sectarian group; it currently amounts to little more than a collection of criminal gangs.[25]

Inter-Ethnic Violence: The Muttehida Qaumi Movement

Another important conflict that has been waged within Karachi and increasingly in other environs has been the violence among the Muhajirs[26] and other ethnic communities such as the Sindhis, Pathans, and Punjabis. Altaf Hussain, a leader among the Muhajir community, founded two organizations to challenge the official and unofficial discrimination faced by his community: the All Pakistan Muhajir Students Organization in 1978 and the Muhajir Qaumi Movement[27] (MQM) six years later in 1984.

In 1992, with active encouragement from the Pakistan army, the MQM split. One faction became the MQM-A (for Altaf) and the second became the MQM-H (Haqqiqi, which means "true" in Urdu). These two factions have episodically targeted one another in competition for influence among the Muhajir community. These internecine conflicts have had bloody consequences and have resulted in significant collateral injury to innocent bystanders. This interfactional violence was most intense during 1993 and 1994. In addition to the fighting between its factions, the MQM also fights with other ethnic groups such as the Jeay-Sindh Movement (which fights for the rights of ethnic Sindhis) as well as with Punjab and Pakhtun militant organizations.[28]

---

[25] Ibid.

[26] Ibid.

[27] The name translates as the Muhajir National Movement. Because Muhajir translates as "refugee" or "migrant," many in Pakistan criticized the continued use of the word to describe the community, despite the numerous generations that have been born in Pakistan and despite the fact that all are Pakistani citizens. In the late 1990s, the organization officially changed its name to the Mutehada Qaumi Movement, to deflect this criticism. Mutehada means "unified."

[28] See *Jane's World Insurgency and Terrorism,* Vol. 17, "Mutahida Qaumi Movement (MQM-A)," February 14, 2003, available at www.janes.com. See also Haq (1995), Shah (1998), and Davis (1996b).

The MQM seeks to wrest control of Sindh from its traditional landed elite and to end the Punjab's perceived domination over the province. The group's hostility toward the Punjab is manifested by the numbers of Punjabi laborers that it has killed. The MQM also wants to establish a high degree of autonomy for Sindh and to establish within Sindh an official homeland for Pakistan's 30 million Muhajirs, most of whom are concentrated in the Sindh cities of Karachi, Hyderabad, Sukkur, and Mirpukhas). The MQM is opposed to the various radicalized Wahhabi and Deobandi Islamic groups that have emerged throughout Pakistan.[29]

The MQM's modus operandi includes instigating riots in Karachi and other key urban centers and calling strikes to bring economic activities in targeted cities to a halt. Karachi is the most vulnerable to such actions, as it is Pakistan's commercial and economic hub. In one of the worst episodes of MQM-incited riots in the mid-1980s, some 120 persons were killed in riots protesting the arrest of Altaf Hussain. The organization has participated in electoral politics, despite its use of terrorism and violence, as political instruments to put pressure on the provincial and central governments. The MQM also assassinates leaders from rival organizations as well as members of the media who are critical of its activities.[30]

The MQM has putative political and militant wings, which can be simplistically compared to the Irish Republican Army (IRA) and Sinn Fein. Its "political" wing comprises a number of sophisticated and articulate politicians who have won seats in the national and provincial assembly as well as at the municipal level. Its "military" wing is a bit blurred, as it is often difficult to distinguish between an activist and a gunman. The city of Karachi is divided into 37 geographic sectors, within which activists are grouped into 10-man units.[31]

---

[29] Ibid.

[30] Ibid.

[31] Davis (1996b).

Figure 4.1
Map of Pakistan

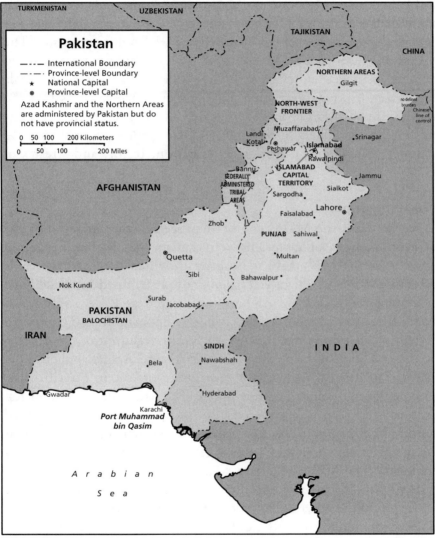

TURKMENISTAN

UZBEKISTAN

TAJIKISTAN

CHINA

Pakistan

— - — International Boundary
— - — · Province-level Boundary
★   National Capital
⊛   Province-level Capital

Azad Kashmir and the Northern Areas
are administered by Pakistan but do
not have provincial status.

0   50 100   200 Kilometers

0   50   100   200 Miles

NORTHERN AREAS
Gilgit

no defined
boundary
Chinese
line of
control

NORTH-WEST
FRONTIER

Muzaffarabad

Srinagar

Landi
Kotal

Peshawar   Islamabad

Rawalpindi

Jammu

Bannu
FEDERALLY
ADMINISTERED
TRIBAL
AREAS

ISLAMABAD
CAPITAL
TERRITORY

AFGHANISTAN

Sargodha

Sialkot

Faisalabad

Lahore

Zhob

PUNJAB   Sahiwal

Quetta

Multan

Sibi

Bahawalpur

Nok Kundi

Surab

Jacobabad

PAKISTAN
BALOCHISTAN

IRAN

SINDH

INDIA

Nawabshah

Bela

Gwadar

Hyderabad

Karachi
Port Muhammad
bin Qasim

A r a b i a n
S e a

MQM's weapons tend to consist of various small arms—mostly from the Afghan arms bazaars of the Northwest Frontier Province and Baluchistan. There are also a number of homemade weapons that are available in the tribal arms factories near Peshawar. The weapon of choice is a Chinese replica of the Russian TT automatic pistol. The MQM also uses an assortment of AK series weapons and a growing number of rocket launchers and Chinese light machine guns. While this inventory may seem menacing, the evidence suggests that the group's use of rocket-propelled grenade launchers has been inaccurate and ineffective. The MQM is most reliant upon actions that it can conduct competently, such as assassination, terror, and street violence.[32]

Violent Synergies

In recent years, the MQM conflict has been further nuanced by the twin phenomena of increasing sectarianism and Pathan migration (mostly from the Northwest Frontier Province) to Karachi that is rendering it a "Pathan" city. This migration stemmed from the flood of Pathan refugees from Afghanistan as well as Pathan relocation from other areas of Pakistan for economic opportunities. The Pathan migrants had robust ties to militant Sunni organizations and benefited tremendously from the various Pakistani Afghan policies that privileged Pathans. As Pathans became ascendant in Karachi, they became natural political competitors to the Muhajirs who claim Karachi as their own. With the onset of sectarian and MQM-inspired conflict in the mid-1980s, Pathans advanced their interests through the financial networks that were developed to support deepening sectarianism. The Muhajir-Pathan conflict was easily given a sectarian veneer by the Pathans due to the preponderance of Shi'a among the leadership of the MQM. "By redefining the axis of conflict in Karachi as sectarian, rather than ethnic, Pathans hope[d] to reduce resistance to their growing political and economic presence."[33]

---

[32] Ibid.

[33] Nasr (January 2000), pp. 183–184.

Karachi, Pakistan's economic hub, was an important theater of operations for the terrorist and syndicated criminal outfits that turned the city into an urban battlefield in the early 1980s. The activities of these organizations were often so intense that the entire province of Sindh was paralyzed. Disillusionment with the law enforcement entities further exacerbated the problem as Karachi's residents ceased seeking assistance from the police. In the early 1990s, the decay of law and order in Karachi became so intense that the army had to step in. This effort was known as "Operation Cleanup." Operation Cleanup will comprise one of the cases examined here.

Pakistan's Force Structure

Pakistan's defense planners tend to view their national security in the context of the Indo-Pakistan dispute. However, most analysts of Pakistan concur that despite the various unresolved issues with its large neighbor to the east, Pakistan's most serious sources of instability come from within—several of which were described above. Pakistan's internal security is further compromised by a wide availability of weaponry, expansive criminal syndicates, weak law enforcement, a paucity of forensic and investigative capabilities, and a crippled and corrupted judiciary.

The regular Pakistan army has about 550,000 persons and another 500,000 in the army reserve. In Pakistan, the army has tended to become involved in internal security duties only as a last resort. Its last intervention in Karachi was Operation Cleanup. Pakistan also has around 100,000 persons employed in various paramilitary capacities under the Ministry of the Interior in peacetime. The paramilitary organization, the Rangers, is deployed for ordinary internal security duties. The Rangers consist of some 25,000 lightly armed troops commanded by officers seconded from the army. While the Rangers force was conceived as a border security force, at present there are some 7,000 Rangers deployed in urban duties—mostly in Karachi.[34]

---

[34] See "Army Organization," *Jane's World Armies*, Vol. 12, June 17, 2002, available at www.janes.com. In the same volume, see "Current Developments and Recent Operations."

Pakistan's four provinces maintain their own provincial police forces. These forces are independent of one another and take guidance from the federal government only when national security is involved. Each of these provincial forces is overseen by an inspector general (IG) who in turn reports to the Ministry of the Interior. The IG has a number of deputies who oversee police affairs within designated sectors of the province. The most important link in implementing police policy is the office of the district superintendent. Constables (police officers) in Pakistan are poorly trained and have low educational attainment. Constables are compensated similarly to an unskilled laborer in Pakistan. Large conurbations tend to maintain their own force, and these forces fall within a provincial chain of command.[35]

Karachi, one of the case studies taken for this chapter, has a police force that numbers some 27,000. There has been discussion of augmenting this police force with another 5,000 personnel as well as establishing a special police force in Sindh province. This new force would number around 2,000 and would be made up of retired army personnel on a contract basis. There has also been discussion of introducing an independent metropolitan police force for Karachi. This would be an effort toward reforming the current police structure, which is seen as "corrupt, slovenly, brutal, extortionate, ill-paid and over-burdened."[36]

The Cases

Operation Cleanup and Its Sequels

The Pakistan army does not have a publishing tradition and tends to publish few critical analyses of its own operations. Our literature review of Pakistan's defense publications identified only a handful of

---

[35] "Security and Foreign Forces, Pakistan," *Jane's Sentinel Security Assessment—South Asia,* January 13, 2002, available at www.janes.com.

[36] "Current Developments and Recent Operations," *Jane's World Armies,* Vol. 12, June 17, 2002, available at www.janes.com.

analyses of Operation Cleanup. All tended to be uncritical of the operation's planning, execution, and impacts.[37] The social science literature has been more analytical in its evaluation of the operation, and this is the literature from which this section draws. Specifically, Azhar Hassan Nadeem (2002) has written one of the most useful treatises on the political economy of lawlessness in Pakistan and discusses this operation's strengths and weaknesses in considerable detail.[38]

The situation in Karachi became particularly acute when the MQM intensified its activities in the mid-1980s. The breakdown of law and order was further exacerbated by the MQM's sweep of local elections in 1986–87. The MQM consolidated its political position by winning all 14 national assembly seats from the urban areas of Sindh. Initially, much of the violence that followed the elections was *against* the Muhajir community, which compelled it to take up armed resistance.[39] According to many accounts, Karachi residents felt that neither their property nor their persons were safe. The city established a series of enclaves that were heavily guarded and gated. As a result of a situation that rapidly spiraled out of control, the federal government entrusted the army to regain and maintain law and order.[40]

While the Pakistani defense literature applauds the army's performance, others such as Nadeem (2002), Ahmar (1996), and Haq (1995) have been very critical. These writers generally agree that Operation Cleanup adversely affected the citizens and degraded the public confidence in the army and the government. The operation resulted in a "prolonged confrontation in which an urban guerilla war was fought in the streets and lanes of Karachi."[41] At the peak of the MQM agitation, its use of rocket launchers against the security forces and state installations became commonplace. The government had to

---

[37] See Naqvi (1994), Ahmad (1999), and Sehgal (1999).

[38] Nadeem (2002).

[39] Ibid., p. 115.

[40] Ibid., p. 116; Davis (1996b).

[41] Ahmar (1996), p. 1034.

draw in law enforcement reserves from other provinces to deal with a highly effective and well-trained urban adversary.[42]

As the situation continued to worsen, the army was withdrawn and the paramilitary force, the Rangers, was deployed in an attempt to control the city. The Rangers entered the city endowed with police powers. Still, there was no effective letup in the violence.[43] 1995 in particular was a terrible year for Karachi: Terrorists attacked a van with personnel from the U.S. Consulate in broad daylight at a busy intersection. Two Americans were slain and one was injured. This was the first time that foreigners were targeted.[44] Karachi's level of violence invited comparison to Beirut and Mogadishu.[45] Ahmar argues that once the paramilitary and police forces took over, the city's condition worsened.

There were numerous long-term consequences from the operation and the subsequent involvement of the paramilitary and police organizations in the fight against the urban guerillas, many of which persist to date. First, the constant war-like situation and the ensuing loss of life alienated urban Sindh from the government in Islamabad. Second, the army was widely seen as a party to the conflict and as perpetrating a state-sponsored genocide against the Muhajir community.[46] Curiously, the army's operations in *rural areas* to establish law and order were not nearly as poorly received as its operations in Karachi, where the army was subject to numerous allegations of excesses, partisanship, and other abuses. Third, Muhajir-related violence increased as a result of the operation.

---

[42] Ibid.

[43] The long-term deployment of the Rangers in Karachi has not been generally well received, at least in part because of their corruption and other problems attendant with the way they exercise authority. For an account of the most recent deployment, see Askari and Hasan (2003).

[44] See Nadeem (2002), pp. 128–129; Ahmar (1996), p. 1044.

[45] Davis (1996b).

[46] For example, the MQM accused the security forces of killing 50 of its workers in February 1996 and another 130 in 1995. The government denied that it engaged in extrajudicial killing and in turn blamed the MQM for the pervasive violence. See Bakhtiar (1996).

Once the MQM-H split from the MQM-A at the army's insti-
gation, both factions fought for dominance and influence among the
Muhajir community and within the government. The MQM factions
used blackmail and coercion to collect revenue and, when such demands were not met, killed innocent persons to retain their coercive
capabilities. This MQM-A/H infighting contributed significantly to
the degradation of Karachi's security and helped create a perception
that the state authorities were incapable of protecting the people's
interests.[47]

Apart from stimulating an escalation of MQM violence, the
army's encouragement of the formation of the MQM-H was imprudent for another set of reasons. With the army's active assistance, the
MQM-H sought to delegitimize the MQM-A by portraying it as a
terrorist organization among the Muhajir community. It conducted
well-publicized tours of the "torture cells" that the MQM-A allegedly
used to intimidate and harm its opponents. This campaign of defa-
mation was done with the active support of the army. This was an
imprudent strategy because it fundamentally delegitimized the
Haqqiqi faction among the preponderance of MQM supporters who
saw the Haqqiqi as "traitors" or "dissidents." Because the Haqqiqi
became widely perceived as a puppet of the army, there was no hope
of transforming the MQM-H into a credible yet more moderate organization that would forswear the use of violence in the pursuit of its
political objectives. Instead, the army's strategy resulted in a faction,
MQM-H, with no support base; a further entrenched MQM-A organization with an effective leader galvanizing the movement from his
"exile" in the United Kingdom; and violent sequences of between-
faction vendetta killings and their resulting human and economic
collateral damage.[48]

Nadeem's criticism of the operation was that it attempted to
solve by military means a problem that was driven by socioeconomic
conditions and changing demographics. Karachi's population has

---

[47] See Nadeem (2002), pp. 120–121, 124.

[48] Haq (1995), p. 1001.

boomed from less than 1 million in 1947 to over 12 million in 2000.[49] The growth has been caused in part by massive waves of ethnically diverse economic migrants flocking to the metropolis from all over Pakistan. One estimate suggests that around 250,000 people come to Karachi annually. Most are people in their twenties from the Punjab and Northwest Frontier Province seeking jobs.[50] In addition, there are some 2 million illegal aliens in the city, primarily from Afghanistan and Bangladesh.[51]

The army's involvement did not mitigate the underlying politico-ethnic tension and arguably even exacerbated this divide by interfering in the structure of the MQM. The fact that the army sought to weaken the MQM by fostering a split only created an environment worsened by factional fighting. Both the Sindhis and the Muhajir felt as if the army's role was merely a way to sideline the substantive issues of their dispute without providing a meaningful forum for resolving them.[52]

Its involvement in the quagmire of Karachi damaged the army's integrity. Some of its personnel became active parties in the civil mayhem during their two years of duty in Karachi. The citizens of Karachi also began seeing the army as an institution that was torturing and killing individuals in custody or in extrajudicial encounters with no due process and rife with inequities. The insecure environment had remained the same for many of Karachi's residents, only now the culprits were equally likely to be military personnel.[53] It is worth noting that while the army rejects the accuracy of this characterization, the widely negative view of the army's presence in Karachi

---

[49] See United Nations, *World Urbanization Prospects: The 1999 Revision,* Table 5, available at http://www.un.org./esa/population/pubsarchive/urbanization/urbanization.pdf, last accessed September 4, 2003.

[50] See Haq (1995), pp. 994–995.

[51] Davis (1996b).

[52] See Nadeem (2002), pp. 355–357.

[53] Ibid.

attests to its organizational failure to manage public perceptions effectively.[54]

The business community of Pakistan, whose interests were imperiled, began mobilizing against the government. Their approach was "no security, no taxes." To minimize government revenue from their businesses, they stopped purchasing advertisement slots on government-controlled media. Any companies that did not follow suit would face a boycott of their products. They also demanded that the army be brought in *with full powers* rather than the enfeebled powers with which they entered the city during Operation Cleanup.[55]

One of the MQM's strategic successes was its ability to internationalize or externalize the conflict: it successfully made Karachi the target of the international media. Violent events taking place in Karachi contributed to an evolving narrative in which the city of Karachi and its province, Sindh, were cast as sconces of lawlessness and crime. Any group wishing to put pressure on Islamabad needed only to conduct an operation in Karachi to draw the attention of the international media and put pressure on Pakistan's only commercial and financial hub.

Altaf Hussain, who has been in a self-imposed exile in the United Kingdom since 1991, uses Karachi's strategic significance in his organization's international perception management campaign. He has embarrassed the government by writing letters to the UN Secretary-General, Amnesty International, and other international human rights organizations requesting their help in stopping Islamabad's policy of genocide against the Muhajirs in Karachi and in Sindh. He has also used the MQM adherents residing within the Pakistani diaspora to cultivate diplomatic and political support for his objectives. MQM adherents within the United States and United

---

[54] Naqvi (1994), Ahmad (1999), and Sehgal (1999) to various degrees refute the characterization of the army's operations in Karachi.

[55] See Nadeem (2002), pp. 128–129.

Kingdom have assembled large protests when Pakistani leaders make official visits to these countries.[56]

Given the resounding failure of Operation Cleanup, what if anything has worked to pacify this troubled city? Davis (1996b) gives an account of the efforts launched to restore civility in 1996. The home minister, Naseerullah Babar, assumed responsibility for pacifying Karachi in late June of that year. Mohammad Shoaib simultaneously became the deputy inspector general (DIG) of police for Karachi. One of the first innovations of this duo was that Shoaib, who would ordinarily report to the inspector general of police for Sindh, had a direct channel to Babar and, through him, the prime minister and the president. Shoaib took over a force numbering 25,000, 8,000 of whom were dedicated to static guard duty for VIPs. An additional 6,000–7,000 Rangers reinforced the police.[57]

Shoaib first acted to restore morale among the police through a series of meetings with the rank and file to discuss grievances. Many of the concerns voiced at this time had to do with the perception that leadership and promotions were not granted on the basis of merit. Within three months, 80 percent of Karachi's 100 station house officers (e.g., heads of police stations) were transferred, and the ensuing replacements were board-selected on the basis of merit rather than the prevailing system of recommendation. (In Urdu, this system of recommendation is known as "safarish" and is widely understood to imply "pulling strings," quid pro quos, or outright bribery to obtain a desired position.) The new station house officers were put on probation with the orders "to lead" or "to quit."[58]

The widespread violence and pervasive distrust of the police and law enforcement agencies had resulted in a dearth of intelligence. Restoring the ability to collect intelligence was another priority of the new DIG. Shoaib did much to ensure that there was greater formalized coordination across the various intelligence agencies that had of-

---

[56] Ahmar (1996), p. 1046.

[57] Davis (1996b).

[58] Ibid.

ten worked at cross-purposes (e.g., the Federal Intelligence Bureau, the military Inter-Services Intelligence Directorate, Ranger Intelligence, the provincial police Special Branch, and local police). Obtaining credible intelligence also required Shoaib to restore public confidence in the state security apparatus. The new DIG attempted to do so by addressing the widespread belief that that the police were corrupt and inefficient. He set up a results-oriented Police Complaints Authority to demonstrate intent to restore the institutional credibility of the police. The Police Complaints Authority resulted in the dismissal of 800 police and criminal charges pressed against another 150 personnel.[59]

In addition to generating better leads among civilians, the police had to cultivate technical means to gather and process intelligence. Under the new DIG, the police banned the use of mobile phones and pagers in order to disrupt MQM communications and force operatives to use landlines, which were often tapped.[60] Unfortunately, Davis does not elaborate on precisely how thoroughly such a ban was enforced and with what means and resources.

The Karachi police bought informants to enhance street-level intelligence collection, even though the quality of that evidence was questionable. The security forces, using these operatives, used the "cordon and search" method in which joint police/Ranger teams would cordon off Muhajir localities in the predawn hours. The teams would round up massive numbers of able-bodied males who would next be paraded in front of turned militants and informants. Between July 1995 and March 1996, Davis reports that some 75,000 Muhajirs were detained in this way.[61] Such actions are a notorious means for the informant to settle scores with his adversaries.

What began as a somewhat successful measure eventually failed in virtually all of its objectives in the end. These coercive measures did produce a level of tactical success in conveying to militants and

---

[59] Ibid.

[60] Ibid.

[61] Ibid.

potential militants that there would be a price paid for these activities. Men who were targeted by the authorities either had to leave their neighborhoods or Karachi altogether. Despite its tactical successes, this effort too was a strategic failure. The methods used were widely seen as repressive tactics and little more than opportunities for official extortion of those rounded up and detained. Many saw these actions as tantamount to a policy of collective humiliation and punishment of communities that supported MQM activities.[62]

Community Policing: An Experiment

Azhar Nadeem (2002) provides an insightful account of a community-policing experiment that was executed while he was the DIG of the Gujranwala Division in 1991. This division is thickly populated and is inhabited by some 10 million residents. Gujranwala District is named after the largest city in this Punjabi district, a city with a population of about 1.2 million.[63]

Nadeem explains the need for a community policing model in Pakistan in the following manner. First, the police forces in Pakistan are resource deprived due to a number of factors, including the burgeoning population, government corruption, enormous public debt, and slow economic growth. (One could add to this list poor tax collection, enormous allocation to the Pakistan armed forces, and overall lack of commitment to the public sector.) Second, effectively augmenting police resources with the communities' human resources may enhance policing quality with less budgetary pressure. Third, information emerging from the public is vital to police efforts to resolve crime.[64]

Nadeem draws from the experience of police forces in England and Wales that give prominence to public involvement and community-based policing in their crime-prevention efforts. This system is

---

[62] Ibid.

[63] See the data at http://www.gujranwalacity.com/popul.php, last accessed September 5, 2003.

[64] Nadeem (2002), pp. 216–217.

further backed by several other institutional structures such as multi-agency policing, organizations for community outreach and education to prevent crime, and other police-initiated forums for community-based policing efforts. Nadeem also draws from the experience of the Metropolitan Police in the 1980s that developed an enlarged media presence and expanded its public relations function. Nadeem was struck by the conflict and hostility between the police and the populace, particularly when seen in contrast to the relationship between the British police and their communities.[65]

Nadeem posits several reasons for the hostility and distrust that permeates the police/policed relationship in Pakistan. First, under colonial rule, the police were the instrument of oppression and dominance and therefore were policing without the consent of the policed. Second, upon independence the police organizations did not evolve in a way that was seen as legitimate by the people. Third, because the police forces continue to be seen as socially and politically oppressive, there is little scope for them to perform protective duties.[66] The author would also add from her considerable in-country experience that the police in Pakistan are structurally underpaid. The compensation of the police forces creates a number of incentives for police to engage in unethical behavior such as extortion, bribery, and demand for "protection money" to discourage police harassment.

Because the police lack legitimacy among the people, information is not given freely. It is more often than not involuntarily extracted. This has further fostered the perception that police forces badger the public. The police also use paid informants who may use their relationship with the police to harass their opponents. The police additionally use random stops on the streets, raiding premises, or taking people in for questioning. Not only does this system produce questionable intelligence, it also alienates the public and fosters the cycle of unwillingness to cooperate with the police and the presumed need for coercion.

---

[65] Ibid., p. 218.

[66] Ibid., p. 219.

The Concept of Community Policing in Pakistan. The basic tenet of community policing is controlling crime with the willing consent of the public. In putting forth this concept for Pakistan, Nadeem is drawing from the basic set of ideas established by Alderson (1981)[67] and innovating to fit Pakistan's unique social and political environment. There are several instruments of community policing that Nadeem identified in this adaptation:

- **Liaisons with representatives of the national and provincial assemblies.** The support of these elected officials can play an important role in ending old rivalries that are often the root cause of ongoing vendetta killings. It is also important to keep them informed of the problems facing their constituents to ensure that they support the functions of the police.
- **Collaboration with local bodies.** Working with local bodies may be important in improving traffic problems and other such public nuisances.
- **Cooperation between the police and the Ulema.**[68] The Ulema may be an important ally in dealing with religious-based crimes such as sectarian violence. Particular times of the month when members of specific sects participate in processions can easily become flash points. Ulema can be brought into "local peace committees" and should come from various sects to try to mitigate sectarian conflicts. Also, the Ulema may be an important partner in dealing with drug addiction and other social crimes.
- **Neighborhood watches.** This involves the close interaction between policemen assigned to particular beats and the citizens of that area. The notion animating this relationship is that both the police and the residents become partners in ensuring safe commercial and residential areas. A number of social organizations can be formed from this relationship: forums to determine public priorities, public awareness programs (e.g., regarding emer-

---

[67] Alderson (1981), cited by Nadeem (2002), p. 222.

[68] The Ulema are religious leaders. Each Muslim sect will have such religious authorities.

gency telephone numbers, ambulance services), and prevention of the unauthorized use of firearms.

- **Citizen/police advisory councils.** This relationship can foster close working relations between the police and the citizens. Councils can also help conduct surveys to evaluate public perceptions of their safety and the performance of the police.
- **Police operations in emergencies.** The police can and should help citizens during floods and earthquakes—not only to provide assistance to the needy but to preclude opportunistic criminal activities at such times.
- **Police conduct.** Police conduct and the public's perception of the police must be improved. Currently, officers are seen as ill mannered, corrupt, and unsympathetic to the plight of the citizens. The police must evolve into partners in law enforcement rather than a corrupt paramilitary force that coerces the public.
- **School involvement.** This is a crucial link to ensure that a new generation grows up to see the police much differently than their parents do. Police who are well received by the youth may be able to offer guidance about drug addiction, civic duties, and ways to combat child abuse. Nadeem also recommends educating children about the law and police in the school curriculum. Police should also better use the media to engage the younger generation.[69]

Experiment and the Results in Gujranwala. Nadeem implemented this experiment in the district of Gujranwala from August 3, 1991 to August 1, 1993. One neighborhood, where the "Neighborhood Watch Programme" was instituted on June 20, 1992, was surveyed twice to evaluate the impact of the police reform efforts. The first survey preceded the launch of the program, gathering information on the residents' perception of their social responsibilities, security requirements, fear of crime, beliefs about police and their legitimacy, and other such issues. The same questions were fielded in

---

[69] Nadeem (2002), pp. 224–227.

January 1993, six months after program launch. The surveys were given to 200 residents of the targeted neighborhood under the auspices of the Citizens Police Advisory Council.[70]

In the first survey, 90 percent of the respondents were not satisfied with the system of police patrolling. In the second, 92 percent were satisfied with the system. Before the program began, only 11 percent of the respondents knew the telephone emergency numbers for the police emergency or their local station. In contrast, 92 percent knew the emergency numbers during the second survey. Similarly, only 49 percent knew that they had a right to request a copy of the "First Information Report" that they registered, compared to 93 percent six months later. Generally, across a broad range of metrics, satisfaction with the police system and perceptions of safety increased among the respondents.

After the program was instituted, residents witnessing a crime indicated an increased willingness to report it to the police (13 percent said that they would report in June versus 91 percent in January). They also registered an increased propensity to give evidence against a known criminal (95 percent said they would not report in June versus 11 percent in January). Residents were also more aware of their environment after the program: In June, 44 percent indicated that they would rent property to a person about whom they knew nothing, compared to 9 percent in January. Residents were also more likely to take common-sense initiatives to reduce victimization (locking doors, verifying strangers at the door before opening it, using a lit bulb outside at night, etc.).

This approach does offer a number of insights for the U.S. government and armed forces in particular. First, many of the internal security dynamics that Pakistan confronts exist in areas where U.S. armed forces have operated, are operating, or will operate. Nadeem's approach offers a methodology whereby a practice that has its origins in the "west" can be adapted to a different environment in ways that reflect the particulars of the culture and society in question. One of

---

[70] Ibid., p. 337. Unfortunately, there is not a wealth of information about how the sample was constructed, whether the two surveys were conducted on the same samples, etc.

the more interesting innovations that may be of use to the U.S. government and its armed forces is the relationship between the police and the Ulema of the various key religious organizations as a first step in mitigating concerns or conflicts arising from religious and sectarian differences.

Summary

While the militant groups engaging in urban campaigns of violence that comprise the subject of this inquiry have not demonstrated excessive innovation, the security forces have not been able to competently counter them. This is most likely due to the inadequate training and resources available to the local police, the corruption and lack of transparency that pervades all of Pakistan's law enforcement and judiciary institutions, the immense distrust between the police and the policed, and the deficient intelligence-sharing apparatuses among state and federal law enforcement and intelligence agencies.

However, Nadeem's community-policing experiment and Operation Cleanup and its sequelae offer a number of insights—however limited—into conducting police operations in a society that is rife with sectarian and ethnic differences. Given the public perception that the police are an occupying force operating without the consent of the population, many police activities have only exacerbated the gulf between the people and themselves. For example, the cordon and search method in Karachi proved to be humiliating to the residents and has been counterproductive because it exacerbated the public distrust of the security forces and provided a system whereby individuals could manipulate the security apparatus to execute vendettas against their rivals.

Pakistan's experience with urban violence is instructive for a number of reasons and should focus the attention of U.S. policymakers. First, the United States is currently operating (albeit with a small footprint) in Pakistan and is relying upon Pakistan to be a capable partner in the war on terrorism. The United States also wants Pakistan to minimize provocative behavior toward India that will increase the likelihood of conflict with that state. Unfortunately, sectarian violence and other internal security threats destabilize Pakistan and interact synergistically with Pakistan-based militant outfits operating in Indian-held Kashmir and beyond in India's hinterland. A nuanced view of Pakistan's internal dynamics must inform U.S. expectations of this government on all fronts. Second, as the Pakistan armed forces and security organizations are currently partners in the U.S.-led war on terrorism, the corruption of these forces, their lack of credibility among Pakistanis, as well as their inadequate training and resources should be of concern. The United States has recognized these problems and has made a number of investments since 9/11 to fortify Pakistan's internal security apparatus.[71] However, more work needs to be done, and the efficacy of these programs should be analyzed to identify the strengths and weakness of the current efforts and suggest further avenues of improvement.

---

[71] See Chalk and Fair (2003).

CHAPTER FIVE

Conclusions

Structural Similarities: Insights for the War on Terrorism

A number of common features emerge across these varied cases. Nearly every group discussed operates on a transnational scale to varying degrees. Even Pakistan's sectarian and anti-state groups with limited political objectives obtain funding and support from states in the Gulf region or from their expatriate communities throughout the world. These transnational networks are effective for the movement of money, persons, and a host of other resources around the globe. These financial networks have become, justifiably, a major focus in the war on terrorism, and degrading them is understood to be critical to disrupting the ability of organizations to finance, man, plan, and execute terrorist strikes.

The transnational presence of militant organizations and their adherents has also permitted groups to interact and cross-fertilize. Afghanistan, the Middle East, India, Europe, Southeast Asia, the United Kingdom, and the United States have all served as meeting places for these militant organizations. The cross-fertilization of militant groups underscores the importance of understanding the best practices of terror utilization, as other groups employing terror are likely to take advantage of this knowledge.

These networks serve to influence relevant co-ethnics and co-religionists throughout the diaspora and encourage them to espouse a particular movement's cause. Diasporas and the institutions they forge are instrumental to the creation of a political environment favorable to the movement's objectives. Such organizations are capable of influencing the political culture of the "host countries" through lobbying and through creating political, cultural, and social institutions that shape the ways in which conflicts are depicted within various media. The university is an important institution for these efforts, as diasporan communities have found ways of controlling the means of knowledge production about themselves and the political goals they pursue.

While the international community understands the financial aspects of these networks, it less clear how much attention other dimensions receive. It is important that counterterrorist activities focus on the presence of these groups and their sympathetic organizations and individuals as well as the primary theater of their operations.

The universities appear to be important because they provide sources of manpower—both foot soldiers and ideologues. The university is also useful because it provides access to individuals with technical expertise who may be tapped voluntarily or through coercion. This is also an important observation—particularly for countries such as Pakistan. The prevalent understanding is that militants in Pakistan draw disproportionately from the religious schools, the madrassahs. If the universities are also sources of militant manpower and resources, they too must comprise a focus of policy attention.

Groups employing terror have tended to use crime to support their activities and the lifestyle of the leadership. In some cases, the criminal networks that they develop are so robust that they resemble transnational criminal syndicates. In other cases, the militant organizations collaborate with or operate through such criminal outfits. This suggests that a law enforcement approach that sees the phenomena of terrorism and organized crime as entirely separate may not be well situated to succeed. The experiences enumerated in this report suggest that law enforcement responses should see these forms of criminal activity as potentially highly correlated.

In many cases in this study, militant groups have exploited the lack of communication and intelligence sharing across jurisdictional lines. This has enabled them to act with relative impunity. Limiting their capability to project power demands a coherent response that includes national and local law enforcement and intelligence entities.

Intelligence utilization is more likely to be optimized by security forces if there are institutional arrangements to permit the flow of intelligence up and down and between national and local authorities as well as movement horizontally among concerned agencies.

The language problem that confronts the Sri Lankan government is noteworthy. The United States has a similar problem in that it has relatively limited capabilities in many of the languages that are critical to the war on terrorism. This affects not only operations abroad, but also the monitoring of suspicious groups at home. Diasporan organizations operating in the United States can exploit the fact that the government has few resources to monitor their exchanges in their own languages. The problem is further exacerbated should these groups choose to encrypt their communications.

The three case studies in this report present similar problems with the relations between the police forces and the civilian populations. All three suggest present conditions where the law enforcement situation becomes so ineffective that the state does not appear to be in control, and citizens do not cooperate with the authorities. The populace will decline to work with the security forces out of fear of the militant organizations and disbelief that the authorities can provide protection. While this is unlikely to be a widespread problem in the United States, there may be pockets within the population where this is the case. It is more likely to be a significant problem as the United States attempts to establish civil order in Iraq and Afghanistan.

Security Cooperation: Implications for U.S. Engagement of Sri Lanka, India, and Pakistan

The United States currently has counterterrorism and law enforcement working groups with India and Pakistan.[1] While the United

---

[1] These programs are the "U.S.-Pakistan Joint Working Group on Counterterrorism and Law Enforcement," which has met twice since its inception in February 2002, and the "U.S.-

States does not have a formal program of this sort with Sri Lanka, it has prioritized greater counterterrorism cooperation with this country. For example, Ambassador Taylor (the former U.S. Department of State's coordinator for counterterrorism) visited Colombo in September 2002, at which time he explained that the focus of his trip was "on the integration of intelligence, law enforcement, legal, and diplomatic efforts against terrorism."[2]

All of these areas identified by Taylor (intelligence, law enforcement, legal, and diplomatic efforts) are the subjects of current U.S. engagement with these three states. As the problems identified in this study suggest, they merit continued and perhaps expanded investment. Rehabilitating the internal security and judiciary apparatus of these states is essential to ensure their optimal participation in the global war on terrorism.

The field work for these analyses also suggests that it would be useful to implement monitoring programs to ensure that U.S. investments in these capabilities are having productive results. In-country interviews suggested that elements of this training may not have permanent or lasting impacts. If this is true, some modification in approach may be in order.[3]

All three cases demonstrate that state counterstrategies are hampered by poor coordination across the myriad state and federal agencies. (The United States too faces this complex challenge.) This finding may have relevance to the United States in its partnerships with each of these countries. For example, when the United States engages Pakistan's Inter-Services Intelligence Directorate (ISI), should it encourage representation from relevant police districts? Are these police capable of interacting with U.S. agencies? If not, what training do they need? What are the key agencies that should be engaged by U.S. delegations in their counterterrorism activities with these (and other)

India Counterterrorism Joint Working Group," which has met five times since its inception in January 2000.

[2] See United States Embassy, Sri Lanka (2002).

[3] Chalk and Fair (2003) also found evidence that some of the U.S. programs in Pakistan warrant evaluation.

states? Understanding the country dynamics in question may enable the United States to better identify which agencies should be included in engagement and which agencies should be targeted for training or other programs to enhance their capabilities. Similarly, such an analysis of the internal security situation for each state may also inform which U.S. agencies should be involved in these engagements. (For example, should the United States also include in its engagements local police officers or individuals from police training academies?)

Finally, it is possible that some of the operational lessons learned by these three states encountering their own cases of militancy may have value for U.S. forces as they confront future and current urban challenges. All three represent complex states with richly diverse populations. Some of the empirical evidence garnered from Pakistan's Islamicized community-policing model and Sri Lanka's vigilance committees may offer some insight for U.S. police operations in similarly complex social environments.

Bibliography

"Chronology of LTTE Suicide Attacks," July 24, 2001. Available at http://www.rediff.com/news/2001/jul/24ltte3.htm, last accessed July 1, 2003.

"Chronology of Suicide Bomb Attacks by Tamil Tigers in Sri Lanka," Society for Peace, Unity and Human Rights in Sri Lanka. Available at http://www.spur.asn.au/chronology_of_suicide_bomb_attacks_by_Tamil_Tigers_in_sri_Lanka.htm, last accessed July 1, 2003.

"Fighting Terrorism," *The Dawn,* March 7, 2004.

"The Generals Offer Advice," *The Economist,* Vol. 336, July 8, 1995, p. 32.

"Gleam of Light in Darkest Punjab," *The Economist,* Vol. 307, No. 7545, April 5, 1988, pp. 38–39.

"International Law Enforcement Cooperation Fights Narcoterror: Drug Enforcement Agency Official Testifies Before Senate Committee," May 20, 2003. Available at http://usinfo.state.gov/topical/pol/terror/texts/03052004.htm, last accessed July 3, 2003.

"Merril Appointed Defence Advisor," *The Island,* available at http://origin.island.lk/2002/03/16/news05.html, last accessed September 14, 2003.

"Militants Storm Red Fort in Delhi," Rediff on the Internet, December 22, 2000. Available at http://www.rediff.com/news/2000/dec/22fort1.htm, last accessed September 10, 2003.

Ahmad, Raja Khurshid, "Army and Terrorism in Sindh," *Defence Journal,* February/March 1999, pp. 77–78.

Ahmar, Moonis, "Ethnicity and State Power in Pakistan: The Karachi Crisis," *Asian Survey,* Vol. 36, No. 10 (October 1996), pp. 1031–1048.

Alderson, J., "Community Cops," Letter to the Editor, *New Society,* 1981, p. 207. Cited in Nadeem, 2002.

Aneja, Atul, "Red Fort Attack: The Biggest Challenge to Ceasefire," *The Hindu,* December 24, 2000. Available at http://www.hindu.com/2000/12/24/stories/02240002.htm, last accessed September 10, 2003.

Asghar, Mohammed, and Baqir Sajjad Syed, "Azam Tariq Gunned Down in Islamabad," *The Dawn* (Pakistan), October 7, 2003. Available at http://www.dawn.com/2003/10/07/top6.htm, last accessed March 9, 2004.

Asia Foundation, *Focus on Sri Lanka,* San Francisco, CA: The Asia Foundation, 2001.

Askari, Hussain, and Syed Shoaib Hasan, "Power Rangers," *The Herald,* August 2003, pp. 49–52.

Axel, Brian, *The Nation's Tortured Body: Violence, Representation, and the Formation of a Sikh "Diaspora,"* Durham: Duke University Press, 2001.

Bajpai, Kanti, P. R. Chari, Pervaiz Iqbal Cheema, Stephen P. Cohen, and Sumit Ganguly, *Brasstacks and Beyond,* New Delhi: Manohar Publishers, 1995.

Bakhtiar, Idrees, "Law of the Gun," *Herald* (Karachi), February 1996, pp. 74–75.

Balasingham, Adele, *The Will to Freedom: An Inside View of Tamil Resistance,* Mitcham, England: Fairmax, 2001.

Bandara, Sandaruwan Madduma, *Lionson: Sri Lanka's "Ethnic Conflict,"* Colombo: Sandaruwan Madduma Bandara, 2002.

Barrier, N. Gerald, "Sikh Politics in British Punjab Prior to the Gurdwara Reform Movement," in Joseph T. O'Connell et al. (eds.), *Sikh History and Religion in the Twentieth Century,* Toronto: University of Toronto, 1988.

Bose, Sumantra, *States, Nations, Sovereignty: Sri Lanka, India and the Tamil Eelam Movement,* New Delhi: Sage Publications, 1994.

———, *The Challenge in Kashmir: Democracy, Self-Determination and a Just Peace,* New Delhi: Sage, 1997.

Brar, Lt. General K.S., *Operation Blue Star: The True Story,* New Delhi: UBSPD, 1993.

Brass, Paul, *Language, Religion and Politics in North India,* Cambridge: Cambridge University Press, 1974.

Bullion, Alan J., "The Indian Peace-Keeping Force in Sri Lanka," *International Peacekeeping,* Vol. 1, No. 2 (Summer 1994), pp. 148–159.

Bullion, Sri, "Dreaming of a War-Free Future," *The World Today,* Vol. 58, No. 12 (December 2002), pp. 26–27.

Burton, Paul, and Rob Fanney, "Sikh Separatists," in *Jane's World Insurgency and Terrorism,* Vol. 17, March 7, 2003. Available at www.janes.com.

Bush, Kenneth, "Ethnic Conflict in Sri Lanka," *Conflict Quarterly,* Vol. 10 (Spring 1990), pp. 41–58.

Byman, Daniel, Peter Chalk, Bruce Hoffman, William Grey Rosenau, and David Brannan, *Trends in Outside Support for Insurgent Movements,* Santa Monica, CA: RAND Corporation, 2001.

Camper, Frank, *MERC: The Professional,* New York: Dell Publishing, 1989.

Center for Defense Information, "In the Spotlight: Liberation Tigers of Tamil Eelam (LTTE)," April 19, 2002. Available at http://www.cdi.org/terrorism/ltte-pr.cfm, last accessed July 1, 2003.

Chalk, Peter, "Liberation Tigers of Tamil Eelam's Internal Organization and Operations: A Preliminary Analysis," A Canadian Security Intelligence Service Publication, March 17, 2000. Available at http://www.csis-scrs.gc.ca/eng/comment/com77_e.html, last accessed July 3, 2003.

Chalk, Peter, and C. Christine Fair, "Pakistan Faces Up to Need for Reform," *Jane's Intelligence Review,* September 2003.

Chandran, Suba, "Born to Die: The Black Tigers of the LTTE," Institute of Peace and Conflict Studies, Article no. 599, October 7, 2001. Available at http://www.ipcs.org/ipcs/printArticle.jsp?kValue=599, last accessed July 1, 2003.

Chandraprema, C. A., *The JVP Insurrection 1987–89,* Colombo: Lake House Publishers, 1991.

Clark, Neil, "Peace Talks Could See Off the IMF," *New Statesman,* Vol. 131 (September 16, 2002), p. 16.

Connor, Robert, "Defeating the Modern Asymmetric Threat," MA Thesis completed and submitted to the Naval Postgraduate School, June 2002.

Danewalia, B. S., *Police and Politics in Twentieth Century Punjab,* New Delhi: Ajanta, 1997.

Davis, Anthony, "Asia, The Conflict in Kashmir," *Jane's Intelligence Review,* Vol. 007, No. 001 (January 1, 1995). Available at www.janes.com.

———, "Asia, Tamil Tiger International," *Jane's Intelligence Review,* Vol. 008, Issue 010, October 1, 1996a.

———, "Karachi: Pakistan's Political Time-Bomb," *Jane's Intelligence Review,* Vol. 8, No. 007, July 1, 1996b. Available at www.janes.com.

Deora, Man Singh, *Akali Agitation to Operation Bluestar,* New Delhi: Anmol Publications, 1991.

——— (ed.), *Aftermath of Operation Bluestar,* New Delhi: Anmol Publications, 1992.

De Silva, Manik, "Sri Lanka's Civil War," *Current History,* Vol. 98, No. 632 (December 1999), pp. 428–432.

De Silva, N., *Anti-State Militant Mobilization, Sri Lanka: 1965–1991,* Ann Arbor: UMI Dissertation Services, 1998.

Evans, Alexander, "The Kashmir Insurgency: As Bad as It Gets," *Small Wars and Insurgencies,* Vol. 11, No. 1 (Spring 2000), pp. 69–81.

Fair, C. Christine, "Military Operations in Urban Areas: The Indian Experience," *India Review,* Vol. 2, No. 1 (January 2003).

———, *The Counterterror Coalitions: Cooperation with Pakistan and India,* Santa Monica, CA: RAND Corporation, forthcoming.

———, "India-U.S. Security Cooperation: Prospects and Challenges," in James Mulvenon (ed.), *The USAF and Security Cooperation in Asia: Basing Access, Logistics, Interoperability and Intelligence-Sharing,* Santa Monica, CA: RAND Corporation, forthcoming.

Fenech, Louis E., "The Taunt in Popular Sikh Martyrologies," in Peshaura Singh and N. Gerald Barrier (eds.), *The Transmission of Sikh Heritage in the Diaspora,* New Delhi: Manohar, 1995, pp. 177–190.

Fitzgerald, Valpy, "Global Financial Information, Compliance Incentives and Conflict Funding," Paper presented to the International Conference on Globalization and Self-Determination Movements, hosted by Pomona College, January 21–22, 2003. Available at http://www.

politics.pomona.edu/globalization/HTML/Valpy%20Fitzgerald.doc, last accessed July 4, 2003.

Fox, Richard G., *Lions of the Punjab: Culture in the Making,* Berkeley: University of California Press, 1990.

Ganguly, Sumit, *The Crisis in Kashmir: Portents of War, Hopes of Peace,* Washington D.C.: Woodrow Wilson Center Press, 1997.

Gellner, Ernest, *Nations and Nationalism,* Ithaca: Cornell University Press, 1983.

Gill, K.P.S., "Endgame in Punjab: 1988–1993," *Faultlines*, Vol. 1 (May 1999), pp. 1–72. Available at http://www.satp.org/satporgtp/ publication/faultlines/volume1/Fault1-kpstext.htm.

Glenn, Russell, "Cleansing Polluted Seas: Non-State Threats and the Urban Environment," *Small Wars and Insurgencies*, Vol. 13, No. 2 (Summer 2002).

Goulbourne, Harry, *Ethnicity and Nationalism in Post-Imperial Britain,* Cambridge: Cambridge University Press, 1991.

Grewal, J.S., "Legacies of the Sikh Past for the Twentieth Century," in Joseph T. O'Connell et al. (eds.), *Sikh History and Religion in the Twentieth Century,* Toronto: University of Toronto, 1988.

Gunaratna, Rohan, *War and Peace in Sri Lanka,* Kandy: Institute of Fundamental Studies, 1987.

———, *Indian Intervention in Sri Lanka: The Role of India's Intelligence Agencies,* 2nd ed., Colombo: South Asian Network on Conflict Research, 1994.

———, "International and Regional Implications of the Sri Lankan Tamil Insurgency," December 2, 1998. Available at http://www.ict.org.il/ articles/articledet.cfm?articleid=57, last accessed August 30, 2003.

———, "Bankrupting the Terror Business," *Jane's Intelligence Review,* Vol. 12, No. 8, August 1, 2000a.

———, "The LTTE and Suicide Terrorism," *Frontline*, Vol. 17, Issue 3, (February 5–8, 2000b). Available at http://www.frontlineonnet.com/ fl1703/17031060.htm, last accessed July 1, 2003.

———, "Suicide Terrorism: A Global Threat," *Jane's Intelligence Review*, Vol. 2, No. 4, October 20, 2000c. Available at http://www.janes.

com/security/international_security/news/usscole/jir001020_1_n.shtml, last accessed July 4, 2003.

———, "Transnational Terrorism: Support Networks & Trends," *Faultlines*, Vol. 7 (November 2000d), pp. 1–29.

Gunaratne, Merril, *Dilemma of an Island,* Colombo: Vijitha Yapa Publications, 2001.

Gunasekara, S.L., *A Tragedy of Errors: About Tigers, Talks, Ceasefires and the Proposed Constitution,* Colombo Sinhala Jathika Sangamaya, 2001.

Haq, Farhat, "Rise of the MQM in Pakistan: Politics of Ethnic Mobilization, *Asian Survey,* Vol. 35 (November 1995), pp. 990–1004.

India Express, "U.S. Denies Any Information About LTTE Indulging in Drug Trafficking," March 3, 2001. Available at http://www.indiaexpress.com/news/world/20010303-0.html, last accessed August 29, 2003.

International Crisis Group, "Pakistan: Madrasas, Extremism and the Military," Islamabad/Brussels: ICG Asia Report No. 36, July 29, 2002.

International Policy Institute for Counter-Terrorism, "Liberation Tigers of Tamil Eelam (LTTE)." Available at http://www.ict.org.il/intcr_tcr/orgdet.cfm?orgid=22, last accessed July 1, 2003.

Interpol General Secretariat, "The Hawala Alternative Remittance System and Its Role in Money Laundering," January 2000. Available at http://www.interpol.int/Public/FinancialCrime/MoneyLaundering/hawala/default.asp, last accessed September 21, 2003.

Jalalzai, Musa Khan, *The Sunni-Shia Conflict in Pakistan,* Lahore: Mustafa Waheed Book Traders, 1998.

Jane's Sentinel and Security Assessment, "Security and Foreign Forces: Sri Lanka," May 7, 2003. Available at www.janes.com, last accessed August 31, 2003.

Jane's World Armies, Vol. 12, Pakistan, "Current Developments and Recent Operations," June 17, 2002. Available at www.janes.com.

Jane's World Insurgency and Terrorism, Vol. 15, "Liberation Tigers of Tamil Eelam (LTTE) [Tamil Tigers]," May 22, 2002. Available at www.janes.com, last accessed September 14, 2003.

Jane's World Insurgency and Terrorism, Vol. 16, "Sipha-e-Sahaba," November 21, 2002. Available at www.janes.com.

Jane's World Insurgency and Terrorism, Vol. 17, "Sikh Separatists," March 7, 2003. Available at www.janes.com.

Jayawardhana, Walter, "Air Wing Leader Killed Was Specializing in Suicide Bombing by Micro Light Aircraft," September 27, 2001. Available at http://www.lankaweb.com/news/items01/290901-2.html, last accessed September 14, 2003.

Joshi, Manoj, "On the Razor's Edge: The Liberation Tigers of Tamil Eelam," *Studies in Conflict and Terrorism,* Vol. 19 (January/March 1996), pp. 19–42.

Juergensmeyer, Mark, *Terror in the Mind of God,* Berkeley: University of California Press, 2000.

Kapur, Rajiv A., *Sikh Separatism: The Politics of Faith,* London: Allen and Unwin, 1986.

Kearney, Robert N., "Tension and Conflict in Sri Lanka," *Current History,* Vol. 85 (March 1986), pp. 109–112.

Kitson, Frank, *Low Intensity Operations: Subversion, Insurgency, Peace-keeping,* London: Boston: Faber and Faber, 1991.

Kulandaswamy, M.S., *Sri Lankan Crisis: Anatomy of Ethnicity, Peace, and Security,* New Delhi: Authorspress, 2000.

Kumar, Ram Narayan, *A Complex Denial: Disappearances, Secret Cremations, and the Issue of Truth and Justice in Punjab,* Kathmandu: South Asia Forum for Human Rights, 2001.

Le Billon, Philippe, Jake Sherman, and Marcia Hardwell, "Controlling Resource Flows to Civil Wars: A Review and Analysis of Current Policies and Legal Instruments," Background Paper for the International Peace Academy "Economic Agendas in Civil Wars" Project Conference, *Policies and Practices for Regulating Resource Flows to Armed Conflicts,* Rockefeller Foundation Study and Conference Center, Bellagio, Italy, May 20–24, 2002. Available at http://www.ipacademy.org/PDF_Reports/controlling_resource_flows.pdf, last accessed July 4, 2003.

Leites, N., and C. Wolf, *Rebellion and Authority: An Analytic Essay on Insurgent Conflicts,* Santa Monica, CA: RAND Corporation, 1970.

Madan, Vijay, "Population Terrain—The Neglected Factor of Counter Insurgency Operations," *Indian Defence Review,* Vol. 12, No. 2 (April–June 1997), pp. 7–11.

Mahmood, Cynthia Kepply, *Fighting for Faith and Nation: Dialogues with Sikh Militants,* Philadelphia: University of Pennsylvania Press, 1996.

Malik, Yogendra K., "The Akali Party and Sikh Militancy: Move for Greater Autonomy or Secessionism in Punjab?" *Asian Survey,* Vol. 26 (March 1986), pp. 345–362.

Mann, Gurinder Singh, "Sikh Studies and the Educational Heritage," in John Stratton Hawley and Gurinder Singh Mann (eds.), *Studying the Sikhs: Issues for North America,* Albany: State University of New York, 1993.

Munasinghe, Major General Sarath, *A Soldier's Version: An Account of the On-going Conflict and the Origin of Terrorism in Sri Lanka,* Colombo: Maj. Munasinghe, 2000.

Nadeem, Azhar Hassan, *Pakistan: The Political Economy of Lawlessness,* Karachi: Oxford University Press, 2002.

Naqvi, Lt. Colonel Hamid Hussain, "Army and Sindh's Internal Security," *Pakistan Army Journal,* Vol. 35, No. 3 (Autumn 1994), pp. 59–62.

Nasr, S.V.R., "The Rise of Sunni Militancy in Pakistan: The Changing Role of Islamism and the Ulama in Society and Politics," *Modern Asian Studies,* Vol. 34, No. 1 (2000), pp. 139–180.

Nasr, Vali, "International Politics, Domestic Imperatives, and Identity Mobilization," *Comparative Politics,* Vol. 30, No. 2 (January 2000), pp. 171–190.

Nayar, Nayar, and Khushwant Singh, *Tragedy of Punjab,* New Delhi: Vision Books, 1984.

Nesiah, Devanesan, "The Claim to Self-Determination: A Sri Lankan Tamil Perspective," *South Asia,* Vol. 10, No. 1 (March 2001), pp. 55–71.

Oberoi, Harjot S., "From Ritual to Counter-Ritual: Rethinking the Hindu-Sikh Question, 1884–1915," in Joseph T. O'Connell et al. (eds.), *Sikh History and Religion in the Twentieth Century,* Toronto: University of Toronto, 1988.

———, *The Construction of Religious Boundaries: Culture, Identity and Diversity of the Sikh Tradition,* Oxford: Oxford University Press, 1994.

O'Connell, Joseph T., "Sikh Studies in North America: A Field Guide," in John Stratton Hawley and Gurinder Singh Mann (eds.), *Studying the*

Sikhs: Issues for North America, Albany: State University of New York, 1993.

Pachnanda, Ranjit K., *Terrorism and Response to Terrorist Threat,* New Delhi: UBS Publishers, 2002.

Pape, Robert A., "The Strategic Logic of Suicide Terrorism," *American Political Science Review,* Vol. 20, No. 32 (July 14, 2003), pp. 1–19. Available at http://danieldrezner.com/research/guest/Pape1.pdf.

Perera, Sasanka, "Sri Lanka's South Still Smoulders," *Himal South Asian,* May 1996. Available at http://www.himalmag.com/96may/, last accessed September 20, 2003.

Pettigrew, Joyce J.M., *The Sikhs of the Punjab: Unheard Voices of State and Guerilla Violence,* New Jersey: Zed Books, 1995.

Puri, Harish K., Paramjit Singh Judge, and Jagrup Singh Sekhon, *Terrorism in Punjab: Understanding Grassroots Reality,* New Delhi: Har Anand Publications, 1999.

Rashid, Ahmed, "A House Divided: MQM Agitates to Split Karachi from Sindh," *Far Eastern Economic Review,* Vol. 157 (November 3, 1994), pp. 21–22.

———, "Living with Terror: Government Fails to Reassure Commercial Hub," *Far Eastern Economic Review,* Vol. 158 (October 19, 1995), p. 24.

Reich, Walter (ed.), *Origins of Terrorism: Psychologies, Ideologies, Theologies, States of Mind,* Washington, D.C., Baltimore, London: Woodrow Wilson Center Press, 1998.

Rhode, David, "Is Pakistan Trying Its Best to Stop Terrorism," *International Herald Tribune,* September 10, 2003. Available at http://www.iht.com/articles/109501.html, last accessed September 14, 2003.

Ribeiro, Julio, *Bullet for Bullet: My Life as a Police Officer,* New Delhi, New York: Viking, 1998.

Sahni, Ajai, "Social Science and Contemporary Conflicts: The Challenge of Research on Terrorism," *Faultlines,* Vol. 9 (July 2001), pp. 131–157.

Sambandan, V.S., "Injured, but Undeterred," *Frontline,* Vol. 17, Issue 01 (January 8—21, 2000). Available at http://www.frontlineonnet.com/fl1701/17010240.htm, last accessed July 1, 2003.

Sarkar, Sumita, and Arvind Tiwari, "Combating Organized Crime: A Case Study of Mumbai City," *Faultlines*, Vol. 12 (May 2002), pp. 133–176.

Schmid, Alex P., "The Links Between Transnational Organized Crime and Terrorist Crimes," *Transnational Organized Crime*, Vol. 2, No. 4 (Winter 1996), pp. 40–82.

Schofield, Victoria, *Kashmir in Conflict: India, Pakistan and the Unfinished War*, London, New York: I.B. Taurus, 2000.

———, *Kashmir in the Crossfire*, London: I.B. Taurus, 1996.

Schweitzer, Yoram, "Suicide Terrorism: Development & Characteristics," April 21, 2000. Available at http://www.ict.org.il/articles/articledet. cfm?articleid=112, last accessed July 1, 2003.

Sehgal, Ikram, "Terrorism, Law and Order," *Defence Journal*, January 1999, pp. 52–55.

Shah, Mehtab Ali, "The Emergence of the Muhajir Quami Movement (MQM) in Pakistan and Its Implications for Regional Security," *Round Table*, 1998, pp. 505–519.

Shani, Giorgio, "Beyond Khalistan? The Sikh Diaspora and the International Order," paper presented as part of the panel on Communal Conflict and Self-Determination Movements in the Local-Global Nexus, International Studies Association Annual Convention, March 27, 2002, New Orleans, U.S.A. Available at http://www.isanet.org/noarchive/ shani.html#_ftn14, last accessed September 8, 2003.

Singh, Attar, "The Shiromani Gurdwara Prbandhak Committee and the Politicization of the Sikhs," in Joseph T. O'Connell et al. (eds.), *Sikh History and Religion in the Twentieth Century*, Toronto: University of Toronto, 1988.

Singh, Lt. General Depinder, *The IPKF in Sri Lanka*, 3rd ed., New Delhi: Trishul Publications, 2001.

Singh, Gurharpal, "Punjab Since 1984: Disorder, Order and Legitimacy," *Asian Survey*, Vol. 36 (April 1996), pp. 410–412.

Singh, Prakash, "An Indian Assessment: Low Intensity Conflict and High Intensity Crime," *Faultlines*, Vol. 5 (May 2000), pp. 125–152.

Smith, Chris, "Security and Stability in South Asia—Part 3: The Non-Conventional Security Dimension," *Janes Online*, April 1996.

South Asia Terrorism Portal, "Suicide Killings—An Overview," available at http://www.satp.org/satporgtp/countries/shrilanka/database/suicide_killings.htm, last accessed July 1, 2003.

———, "Prominent Political Leaders Assassinated by the LTTE," 2001, available at http://www.satp.org/satporgtp/countries/shrilanka/database/leaders_assassinated_byLTTE.htm, last accessed July 1, 2003.

Sprinzak, Ehud, "Rational Fanatics," *Foreign Policy*, No. 120 (September/October 2000), pp. 66–73.

Subramanian, Nirupama, "Peace Process Will Move Forward, Says Ranil," *The Hindu*, December 22, 2001.

Swamy, M.R. Narayan, *Tigers of Lanka: From Boys to Guerillas,* Colombo: Vijitha Yapa Publications, 2002.

Tatla, Darshan Singh, "The Punjab Crisis and Sikh Mobilization in Britain," in Rohit Barot (ed.), *Religion and Ethnicity: Minorities and Social Change in the Metropolis*, Kampe, Netherlands: Kok Pharos Publishing House, 1993.

———, *The Sikh Diaspora: The Search for Statehood,* London: UCL Press, 1999.

Telford, Hamish, "The Political Economy of Punjab: Creating Space for Sikh Militancy," *Asian Survey,* Vol. 32, No. 11 (November 1992), pp. 969–987.

Tellis, Ashley J., C. Christine Fair, and Jamison Jo Medby, *Limited Conflicts Under the Nuclear Umbrella: Indian and Pakistani Lessons from the Kargil Crisis,* Santa Monica, CA: RAND Corporation, 2001.

Tully, Mark, and Satish Jacob, *Amritsar: Mrs. Gandhi's Last Battle.* Calcutta: Rupa and Co., 1991.

United Nations, *World Urbanization Prospects: The 1999 Revision,* Table 5. Available at http://www.un.org./esa/population/pubsarchive/urbanization/urbanization.pdf, last accessed September 4, 2003.

United States Department of State Media Note, "Second Annual U.S.-Pakistan Joint Working Group on Counterterrorism and Law Enforcement," April 15, 2003. Available at http://www.state.gov/r/pa/prs/ps/2003/19666.htm, last accessed September 14, 2003.

United States Department of State, "U.S.-Pakistan Joint Group on Counter-terrorism Meets," May 8, 2002. Available at http://usinfo.state. gov/topical/pol/terror/02050908.htm, last accessed September 14, 2003.

United States Embassy, Sri Lanka, Press Release: "U.S. Counterterrorism Coordinator Visits Sri Lanka," September 24, 2002. Available at http://usembassy.state.gov/srilanka/wwwhpr0924a.html, last accessed March 10, 2004.

United States Institutes of Peace, *Simulation on Sri Lanka: Setting the Agenda for Peace.* Available at http://www.usip.org/class/simulations/ srilanka.pdf, last accessed June 25, 2003.

Warrick, Joby, "Iran Admits Foreign Help on Nuclear Facility: U.N. Agency's Data Point to Pakistan as the Source," *Washington Post,* August 27, 2003, p. A17. Available at http://www.washingtonpost.com/ ac2/wp-dyn?pagename=article&node=&contentId=A50470-2003Aug26 &notFound=true, last accessed September 14, 2003.

Whall, Helena, *Assessing the Sri Lanka Peace Process,* paper for the Political Studies Association—UK 50th Conference, London, April 10–13, 2000a.

———, "Ethnonationalism and Receding Cultural Mobilization in Sri Lanka," working paper presented at the 16th European Conference on Modern South Asian Studies, Edinburgh, September 6–9, 2000b. Available at http://www.tamilinfo.org/about_tic/archives/documents/shr/ Helena_Edinburgh.pdf, last accessed June 25, 2003.

Wirsing, Robert G., *India, Pakistan, and the Kashmir Dispute: On Regional Conflict and Its Resolution,* London: Macmillan 1998.

Yaeger, Carl, "Sikh Terrorism in the Struggle for Khalistan," *Terrorism,* Vol. 14, No. 4 (October 1991), pp. 221–231.

Zaman, Muhammad Qasim, "Sectarianism in Pakistan: The Radicalization of Shi'a and Sunni Identities," *Modern Asian Studies,* Vol. 32, No. 3, (1998), pp. 689–716.